THE ETHICAL AND MORAL CODE OF CONFUCIUS

Calixto López
Rosalía Rouco

THE ETHICAL AND MORAL CODE OF CONFUCIUS

CALIXTO LÓPEZ
ROSALÍA ROUCO

(2016)

THE ETHICAL AND MORAL CODE OF CONFUCIUS

FOREWORD

It is common when speaking of the Chinese sage, philosopher and teacher of ancient Kung-Fu-Tsu (Confucius), to refer to him in the previous qualifying terms, with which we overlook the most important facet of this transcendental figure of Eastern culture concerning Ethics and Morals, which in the end were, or are the basic elements of his doctrine and on which Confucianism was formed as an ideological current.

And it is precisely the main objective of Confucian doctrines is to develop in individuals high moral qualities that allow them to relate and live in perfect harmony, enjoying full freedom and welfare regardless of race, sex, or social or economic status.

Hence the meaning of life and the efforts of the genial thinker so that these objectives could be put into practice in any of the special situations in which people found themselves; and the historical panorama that he had to live was extremely hostile in this sense.

But starting from perseverance, study and constant self-improvement, basic elements of his theory, Confucius managed to gather around him a large group of disciples and followers who would ultimately spread his doctrines later, which in the end would reach every corner of the planet, but always starting from the ethical nucleus necessary in the formation of values, which it was necessary for individuals to possess.

For there to be honest subjects and for them to enjoy all rights, including that of education, it was necessary that in correspondence there should be honest, human and honest governors and governments who would set an example and guide the former in progress and well-being, which was ultimately what Confucius aspired to: the well-being and freedom of all men regardless of their social status or caste origin.

Undoubtedly, to achieve that in the conditions of the nascent Asian culture was impossible and of course a utopian task, which earned the illustrious thinker to consider in some moment of vacillation, like the one common in men, that the effort of all his life had been in vain and that he had not been able to carry out his work. Nothing could be further from reality, for he laid the foundations and the path to follow so that one day this would become possible. Incidentally, this has not yet been achieved in any country in the world, although in some nations citizens enjoy greater freedom, rights and welfare than in others, but still far from Confucian objectives and examples need not be mentioned, because anywhere in the world there are inequalities, injustices and helplessness of the most humble, although there are some in which this constitutes *the bread of every day* and reach chilling levels material miseries, human and all kinds.

But in relation to the above, Kung-Fu-Tsu or Confucius, as it was renamed in the West, pointed out the objective, the direction and the sense to follow so that one day the inequalities between human beings will disappear, which in the end, as Mencius added, one of the most eminent followers of Confucius in the fourth classic book: are good by nature and have the possibility of overcoming their deficiencies, errors and defects, to develop high moral and human feelings such as those of kindness, decorum, honesty, honesty and above all those of solidarity and social coexistence, which are those that have enabled the development and progress of man over the other species of the animal kingdom.

To illustrate the above, at the end of the essay have been included, after a careful and rigorous selection, more than 200 aphorisms of Confucius related to one of the most important and transcendental aspects of today's society: ethics and morals. We say important, because the accelerated rhythm with which the productive forces of the globalize world advance has left behind the capitalist productive relations based on the unequal distribution of wealth, according to the role that individuals play in relation to their role as owners or not of the means of production, and since the dominant position is held by the former, this implies that these inequalities cross the economic barrier and directly affect the social superstructure in basic aspects such as politics, education, ethics and morality, among others.

It is precisely about ethics and morality that this essay deals with, taking as its centre the doctrines of Confucius, independently of the fact that they were enunciated more than 2500 years ago, but they have not lost their validity because they are focused precisely on the ethical and moral formation of the individual, through education to prepare him for his corresponding role in society.

It is no secret that the ideals of equality and social equilibrium preached by this illustrious thinker have not yet been achieved in our days; on the contrary, the high tension emanating from the unequal development of the productive forces with respect to the production relations in force, reaches even more dramatic shades in today's globalize world.

The high technological development achieved by society, and the wealth of raw materials on the planet, would make it possible for all individuals to have access to the basic necessities of life: food, housing, education, health and the right to work and culture in general. But this, far from being so, has taken proportions of social inequality incredibly higher than in any other social-historical regime. It is a fact that the rich are getting richer and the poor are getting poorer, and that the former squander the planet's resources and the latter are deprived of the basic means necessary to survive.

Consequently, there is no ethical and moral argument to justify this inequality, which takes on nuances of cruel and inhuman exploitation in many third world countries, and also among different sectors of the population in the developed countries themselves, according to the role they play as owners or not of the means of production.

Government institutions, social organizations, and even religious organizations are deaf to this reality. Some social groups pay little attention to these problems, but they do not have sufficient resources to provide an adequate help or solution to them, which, moreover, far exceed their material and execution possibilities.

As in the time of Confucius, the evils we have analyzed are in force, without the citizens who direct the society paying attention and taking forceful actions for their solution. On the contrary, it is frequent to observe that a significant number of executives of different ranks and levels make a malicious use of ethical values, and divulge and promise actions with the sole fact of reaching power, and once with it, they disregard promises to the dispossessed classes and corrupt themselves by appropriating or wasting the resources and public wealth that are under their custody.

And if public institutions are not capable of addressing the pressing problems of society by practicing a double standard of conduct, then it is necessary to return to the burden with those old thinkers who, like Confucius, did not rest while they lived and dedicated their entire existence to disseminating doctrines of equality and equal social rights for all people, regardless of their social stratum or level of wealth. For this reason, a summarized version of *"The Four Classical Books of Confucius"* is attached at the end of the book, which endorses and expands on the arguments of this modest essay.

THE ETHICAL AND MORAL CODE OF CONFUCIUS

I. INTRODUCTION. OUR TIME

"The courtesy that should preside over our daily actions is based primarily on respect and understanding for all."

How can we behave in this era of globalization where moral norms and principles are conspicuous by their absence when confronted with power, money or capital?

How can we survive as dignified people, with decorum, on the margins of the vices of a civilized but imperfect society?

How can we maintain family unity in such an aggressive social environment?

With what moral weapons can we preserve human values, and fully develop our personality, while facing a hostile social environment?

Many more questions like these can flock to our heads, without us having the right answers for the time being, or we are in a position to tackle these pressing problems of today's society.

We do not pretend then to give secret, magical or wonderful formulas, because for no problem of today's complex society there are remedies or simple solutions. Neither can we fail to tackle the problems because if there is something complex and marvellous it is the human brain, which has so far been victorious in all the battles that man has fought, even though it is physically weaker than any animal it faced at the dawn of human evolution.

It is indisputably a time of crisis of values, and in such circumstances we must fill ourselves with courage, choose the right weapons and face it resolutely. But we are not referring to the classic war weapons, but to the cognitive ones, to the universal experience accumulated by society for more than 10 000 years of social existence of the human being.

From the point of view of the knowledge accumulated by the human being throughout history, it is not difficult to find personalities or geniuses of the intellect, who from one point of view or another have focused on similar problems, either in their time, in the past, or even projected on a distant future.

The list of sages, philosophers, sociologists and intellectuals of various kinds who have dealt with the ethical and moral problems of society throughout history could perhaps be overwhelming, the revision of which would lead us to a job of never finishing what is not advisable for the approach of pressing problems of humanity framed in a concrete historical period of abrupt, dynamic and even sometimes uncontrollable and unpredictable social changes, as is the case for modern society today.

It is advisable, then, to focus on a few of them, or only one of them at the moment, but which has approached human problems from an essentially human point of view, worth the redundancy, where it values positively the essence and nature of man emphasizing the ethical and moral values of man, and the possibility that if he does not bring them together he will be able to reach them or develop them through effort, tenacity, study and constant self-supervision throughout life.

After valuing the works of numerous humanists from antiquity to the present, we opt for one who lived in the East at the dawn of civilization, and whose doctrines have marked, and constitute the basis upon which the ethical and moral values of several Asian countries that have achieved remarkable development in recent times are based, and that their citizens constitute paradigms of seriousness, respect, education and good treatment towards their peers, as well as respect for traditions, the family and the elderly. In essence, we are referring to Confucius and the doctrine created by him: Confucianism.

Because who better to address the current human problem than the Chinese Confucius sage, philosopher and teacher? who lived in a chaotic, disordered epoch of history; in a moment of collapse, of collapse of a millenary dynasty; And yet, in these difficult conditions he was able to impose himself in the midst of corruption, injustices, inequalities, unjust norms of inhuman exploitation of man, and had the genius and courage to proclaim and design a unique ethical and moral doctrine, directed towards the creation of ethical values and principles and towards the integral formation of the people who were to direct society to make it just, humane and focused on the well-being and happiness of people; and where all, regardless of their cradle or social reason, could prepare themselves to play a humane and dignified role in society, and even direct it if necessary.

This illustrious thinker, Confucius, was able to inculcate the ethical values that he proclaimed to his disciples and followers, educating them in his doctrines and moral principles that were to be possessed by all citizens, from the rulers to the individuals of lesser rank, of that society on the verge of its collapse and self-destruction.

Great epochs demand great personalities, men of action with voice, with pen, with thought; courageous at times when a single word or opinion expressed at the wrong time or place can lead them to death. And one of these men was Confucius some 25 centuries ago, practically at the dawn of human civilization.

The Zhou dynasty, in force for more than five centuries, collapsed in the lands of the Celestial Empire, plunged into chaos and disorder, and was Kung-Fu-Tsu: Confucius, orphan of a nobleman who had come at least, who raised the standard of principles, morals and ethical values to guide his people, practically peacefully, subtly and imperceptibly, out of that abyss and face the future; if not by solving all the evils, at least by exposing the necessary and indispensable principles on which the successive Chinese dynasties were based, starting from the fact that every man has the right to education and access to public office, regardless of his social reason, provided that he shows the necessary capacity, tenacity, knowledge and preparation, under a morality and dignified and exemplary conduct in society.

Much of what the highly developed countries of Southeast Asia are: Japan, China, Taiwan, South Korea, Singapore, and the accelerated advance of Vietnam itself, has to do with the ethical doctrines of the remarkable thinker Confucius. And it is not that we decided to refer to Confucianism as a form of government, nor an integral philosophical system, because it covered aspects of the social superstructure and not of the economic base, and not even all aspects, but the basic ones: morals, education and politics. And with these it was enough to contribute to the formation of the statesmen who managed to guide their peoples so that their countries would emerge from a highly backward form of production and achieve the levels of development reached today that are on a par with the most developed western societies.

An illustrious 19th century Cuban thinker, José Martí, politician and hero of the independence struggles of this country, stated something like this: *"where there are men without decorum there are others who carry within themselves the decorum of many"*. And the moral doctrine of Confucius brings together for human beings these ideals of decorum and exemplary conduct, necessary to develop in today's society, without the need to resort to dirty or corrupt methods, lies and disloyalty, betrayal and excessive greed.

One can become a great man by consistently applying the ethical and moral ideas of Confucius without the need to accumulate exorbitant fortunes or wealth. The happiness of the human being can be reached with the balance of the necessary material goods that allow the integral development of the people, without excessive ambitions, and more than to look for the neighbour, to deepen in oneself, in how am I and how should I behave, not in how is he and what does he do?

In the present work we have managed to gather more than 200 aphorisms of Confucius, some may call him maxims, for the moral and cognitive universe that encompass, sentences, famous phrases or as the reader pleases, but thoughts that encompass a teaching and an ideal of conduct useful and necessary to face the challenges of today and the future, and to allow all human beings on the planet to live together in peace, harmony, and spiritually calm and serene, because there are goods and material resources for all; it is only necessary to make good use of them in pursuit of a just cause: **the well-being of all humanity**.

II.-THE NOT CONFUSED ETHICS OF CONFUCIUS.

"He who desires for others what he would desire for himself, and does not do to his fellow men what he would not have them do to him, possesses the righteousness of heart and complies with the standard of moral conduct which his own rational nature imposes on man.

Confucius placed at the centre of his doctrines the problem of ethics and morals, necessary, according to him, to form leaders, officials and other persons who held public and government responsibilities, as well as that those, imbued with these precepts were able to be examples in their daily activity, for the people who directed, or were under his direct or indirect mandate.

Practically we can affirm that moral and ethical principles, and within them the exemplary conduct of the citizens, mainly the rulers, was the heart of the Confucian doctrines, where all the liquid that nourished the different spheres of society was circulated. Rulers who were just, honest and who constantly set an example would deserve, in correspondence, subjects who would equal or emulate them in their actions and in this way a balanced society would be achieved, without the need for revolts or social movements of any kind.

In spite of Confucius' apparently utopian or simplified reasoning, he went further and went so far as to raise, at the very dawn of civilization, the need for that movement to form dignitaries to include not only nobles, or men of fortune, but also any citizen regardless of their origin or social class, regardless of their wealth or poverty.

This new blood would make possible a constant renewal of the social hierarchy preventing the stagnation of castes living in China at the end of the Zhou dynasty, where public posts and government were associated with members of the ruling nobility castes, which prevented motivations and a spirit of improvement and work for them, because whatever happened, whoever was born favoured by his status of nobility knew that he was assured a high public rank, regardless of his preparation and aptitude to govern.

Seen in this way, Confucius established a kind of triangle where each vertex represented one of the basic aspects of the social superstructure, that is: Ethics-Politics-Education, leaving for the latter the important role of forming the moral values of the individual, which at the same time would be embodied in the work of government.

Confucius considered that once properly formed the subjects who would exercise the control and direction of the State everything else would flow spontaneously: the juridical system, the arts, and even the very economic base of society. That is, it would directly influence the mode of production of wealth, distributing it rationally according to the needs and participation of the individual in the production process.

Although the order in which things are presented seems somewhat erroneous, from a Marxist point of view and other materialist philosophical systems, which put the economic base before the social superstructure, it must be recognized that the system was so well elaborated that it worked in the following centuries, mainly in the following Dynasty in the historical order: the Han and has maintained certain validity during thousands of years in the Asian countries, many of which have privileged places in the world socioeconomic development, as we mentioned before.

Of course, it would be a mistake to assume that only with the ideas and doctrine of Confucius would the industrialized countries of Southeast Asia have reached the high levels of current socioeconomic development, but what is certain is that Confucianism has been one of the elements that has contributed to this development of social and economic progress, although it is not completely determinant.

It should also be noted that the doctrines of Confucius, as they have come to our days in the form of dialogues, conversations, questions and answers, have contributed by their simplicity and clarity to keep this thought alive, regardless of the 25 centuries that have passed since the death of the brilliant Chinese thinker.

In contrast to other doctrines that address the problems of ethics, morals, education and politics, that of Confucius is extremely clear, diaphanous, transparent, unlike that of other thinkers who might be confusing to the common man, because of the distance in the time in which they were developed, the personality of their authors, and even some relatively recent. In the ideas of Confucius there is nothing of "confusion", independently that these two words do not have any relation between them, except for those who like the association of terms and consonants of similar pronunciation.

It cannot be said, however, that Confucius made novel contributions to the moral doctrines of the time, but rather that he expressed verbally what the ideal of conduct of citizens would be, even if in practice they were not carried out, and that he failed to acquire a stable position in that distant dynasty of bureaucratic government.

Confucius' ideas were not applied consistently in his time, but by the subsequent dynasties, especially the "Han", which ruled China for four centuries, anchoring itself in the conceptual basis of the Confucian doctrine, which allowed it to reach a high degree of splendour in its relatively long existence.

Confucius' ideal was not to abolish norms, but to regulate what according to his doctrine could help to achieve a harmonious balance in existing social relations and also in family relations, in the respect of children for fathers, from younger brothers to older ones, from wives to their husbands, etc. But, and it is always very important to point out, starting from the fact that those who led the direction fulfilled and were an example in their functions.

There is another of the basic pillars of Confucianism, the "example", taken to its maximum expression by the leaders; without it nothing would be achieved and this could go as far as the justification of rebellion, considered then as a blasphemy, a sin, a dangerous crime to put it on the table in a society in which the most common thing is that nobody maintains an exemplary conduct.

But more than talking about Confucius' moral doctrine, the most important thing is to read, study and deepen each one of his ideas, so we will begin to evaluate with the reader the precepts, thoughts, sentences, or aphorisms as they could be called of this remarkable thinker, and that although they cannot be seen as a magical and definitive solution to the multiple and complex problems of the time, if they represent a useful and adequate guide for those who care about, or occupy themselves with this matter, which I believe **all human beings should be**.

III.-ETHICAL VALUES IN CONFUCIUS APHORISMS.

In a very simplified way we can consider ethical values as guides or norms of conduct that regulate the behaviour of the individual. The way or degree in which these are fulfilled characterizes the human quality of a person in a particular social environment. Among these, the most important are: *justice, freedom, responsibility, integrity, respect, loyalty, honesty, equity, love, solidarity, humanism, consideration*, acceptance, recognition, appreciation, brotherhood, compassion, among others.

Confucius considered, as it is understood in our time, that ethical values are acquired in the development of the human being from birth to death and that they are conditioned to the family and social environment in which it develops. Therefore, no one is born predetermined by nature to show one behaviour, or another.

Confucius' aphorisms or sentences continually address the ethical values of the individual, given his consideration that these could be acquired by anyone, regardless of their social or economic status throughout life, through constant and tenacious self-improvement, and that the subjects who stood out most in this sense (gentlemen) should be those who directed society and assumed the relevant positions of government, in order to achieve a just society for all.

Below are some of these aphorisms associated with the corresponding ethical values:

— Respect and understanding human beings:

The courtesy that should preside over our daily actions is based mainly on respect and understanding for all.

— Equality, reciprocity, love of neighbour:

My doctrine is summed up in one thing: "tchung" (the means); or, perhaps, in one word: "shu" (equality, reciprocity, love of neighbour).

— Reflect:

Reflect calmly before adopting any determination, never tire of doing good, and deal with each matter as appropriate.

— Calm, tranquillity, equilibrium:

A man does not try to see himself in the water that flows, but in the calm water, because only what is calm in itself can give tranquillity to others.

— Discretion, frugal speech:

He who speaks excessively and without sanity rarely puts into practice what he says. The noble man never fears that his words will surpass his deeds.

Silence is the only friend who never betrays.

— Balanced behaviour harmony:

The measure and the means are the culmination of

human nature. The state in which neither hope, nor anger, nor sadness, nor joy is yet manifested, is called the medium. The state in which they manifest themselves but get the right rhythm is called harmony.

— Self-control:

Self-control rarely leads one to make mistakes.

— Honesty:

When you see an honest man, try to imitate him. When you see a man who is not honest, examine yourselves (examine if you have the same defects).

— Fellowship:

When one is in the service of a lord, pettiness attracts misfortune; in friendly relations, pettiness attracts distancing.

— Humanism, benevolence:

Only a benevolent man can love and hate others.

When one seeks to realize humanity, there is no place for evil.

— Virtue:

A man without virtue cannot endure adversity and joy for long. A good man rests in his humanity. A wise man knows how to use it.

— Preach by example:

A superior man can be described as one who first puts his ideas into practice, and then preaches to others what he already does.

— The spiritual in conjunction with the material:

You ask me why I buy rice and flowers? I buy rice to live and flowers to have something to live for.

— Save the measurement:

It is as bad to pass from the measure as not to reach it.

— Non-interference in the life of others:

The greatest defect of men is to worry about removing the weeds from the fields of others, neglecting the cultivation of their own fields.

— Parity in speaking

The nobleman never expresses his opinion about things he does not understand. He seeks maximum precision in his words; this is the most important thing.

— Loving one's neighbour:

He who loves men strengthens men, for he himself wishes to be strengthened; he helps men to achieve success, for he himself wishes to achieve success.

What does goodness consist of? In loving all men.

— Meditation:

The man who does not meditate and act with haste will not be able to avoid great failures. You must always keep your head cool, your heart warm and your hand outstretched.

— Truth as a basic element of human nature:

Truth cannot be separated from human nature. If what we consider truth departs from human nature, then it cannot be true.

— Observance about the behaviour of the others:

Find out a man's reasons for acting, observe how he acts, and examine where he finds peace. Is there anything else he could hide from us?

—Respect for religious values and sincerity in their practices:

If a man has no humanity, what is the use of rites? If a man has no humanity, what is the use of music to him?

— Austerity:

A gentleman eats without filling his belly; he chooses a dwelling without demanding comfort; he is diligent in his work and prudent in his speech; he seeks the company of the virtuous to correct his own conduct. Of such a man one can truly say that he has the desire to learn.

— Embarrassment and virtue:

Driven by political manoeuvres and content with punishments, people become cunning and lose their shame. Driven by virtue and moderated by rites they develop a sense of shame and participation.

— Simplicity and attention to others:

To possess capacity and talents, and to accept the opinion of those who lack them; to have much and to accept the opinion of those who have nothing; to be rich and to behave like being poor; to be full and to seem empty and devoid of everything; to let oneself be offended without manifesting resentment; in another time I had a friend who behaved this way in life.

— Ethical values as a system of closely interlinked elements:

A virtue can never subsist in isolation; it must always be protected by other virtues.

— Responsibility in our actions:

Misfortunes, like fortune, only come when we have sought them through our actions.

— Sincerity, fidelity and good faith in our actions:

If the wise man observes a dismissive behaviour, he will not inspire respect; if he limits himself to studying, his knowledge will not be deep. You must always be sincere, faithful and act in good faith.

— Sincerity against hypocrisy:

An eminent position without nobility of character,

worship without veneration, funerary practices without sincere pain: here are situations I can't stand.

— Ingenuity, simplicity:

The noble man preserves throughout his life the naivety and innocence characteristic of childhood.

— Auto correction:

From the noblest man to the humblest, all have the duty to improve and correct their own being.

— Harmony and balance:

The situation in which we are when joy, pleasure, anger or sadness have not yet developed in our minds is called the "centre". As soon as such passions begin to develop without exceeding a certain limit, we find ourselves in a state called "harmonious" or "balanced". The straight path of the universe is the centre; harmony is its universal and constant law.
When the centre and harmony have reached their highest degree of perfection, peace and order reign in heaven and on earth, and all beings reach their full development.

— Adapt to the circumstances:

The noble man, whatever the circumstances in which he finds himself, adapts to them so that he always remains at the centre. As soon as he obtained a new virtue, he attached himself to it, perfected it within himself and no longer abandoned it in all his life.

— Moral and ethical principles above laws, politics

and everything else:

Much more excellent is the virtue of one who remains faithful to the practice of good, even though the country lacks laws and suffers from poor administration.

— Reciprocity and equality in one's own human conduct and that of others:

He who desires for others what he would wish for himself, and does not do to his fellow men what he would not have them do to him, possesses the righteousness of heart and fulfils the standard of moral conduct which one's own rational nature imposes on man.

— Rationality. Do not act with haste:

If, before we begin to speak, we determine and choose words beforehand, our conversation will not be vacillating or ambiguous. If in all our businesses and companies we determine and plan in advance the stages of implementation, we will easily achieve success. If we determine our standard of conduct in this life sufficiently in advance, at no time will our spirit be assailed by restlessness? If we know our duties beforehand, it will be easy for us to fulfil them.

— Self control:

Control yourself even at home; do not do, even in the most secret place, anything you may be ashamed of.

— Fairness and courage:

To know what is right and not to practice it is cowardice.

— Modesty:

The only thing I aspire to and desire is not to fall into the need to boast about my virtues and my intelligence, and not to proclaim my good deeds.

— Righteousness in words, respect for justice and humanity over riches:

Seek first of all the righteousness of our words, and then adjust our conduct to them. Always work in accordance with justice, to perfect ourselves every day in its realization. Inner anxieties come from wanting the life of those you love, while you want the death of those you could, because that is like wanting someone's life and death at the same time. The perfect man does not place his greatest aspiration in riches.

— Patience, constancy, humility:

The vulgar man is vain and proud, even when his position is not elevated. The man who is constant, patient, humble and measured in speaking is very close to perfection.

— Tolerance before of the defects and vices of others:

Prudence advises not to be indignant when men deceive us, not to be sad when they are unfaithful. The prudent man always foresees these eventualities.

— Meditate and act without haste:

27

The man who does not meditate and act with haste will not be able to avoid great failures.

— Value fairness regardless of where it comes from or who says it:

The nobleman does not give credit to words by the authority of the one who pronounces them; neither does he reject the truth even if it comes from an ignorant person.

— Constancy and patience:

Fickleness and impatience destroy the highest purposes.

— Fairness in valuations:

When the crowd despises someone, you must objectively examine their conduct before giving your opinion. Even when the crowd acclaims someone, it is necessary to contemplate with impartiality their works before approving them.

— Emulate and copy the virtues of others:

Nothing is more worthy of admiration in a noble man than knowing how to accept and imitate the virtues of others.

— Good against evil:

It is necessary for men to know evil in order to be able to avoid it and give themselves to the practice of good.

— Righteousness in action:

I have never heard that a man who did not act uprightly could straighten others. Still less could he make others sincere who observe hypocritical behaviour.

—La human nature and how to perfect it:

Human nature is neither good nor bad. According to this, the goodness or malice of men is something subsequent to human nature itself in its origin. If man possesses the capacity to act, it is necessary that he also possess a norm to direct his acts.

— The search for the right path:

The right way is like a wide avenue; it is not difficult to find it when one seeks it, but men do not strive to discover it.

— Deaf ears to gossip and murmurings of bad faith:
I do not pay the slightest attention to the murmurings and criticisms of men.

— The permanent struggle to achieve goodness:

Is goodness something unattainable? As long as you yearn for goodness, it will be at hand.

— Imperfection of human beings and the struggle to develop principles:

I cannot expect to find a perfect man. I would be content to simply find a man of principles. It is difficult to have principles when Nothing pretends to be Something, Emptiness pretends to be Full and Poverty pretends to be Opulence.*

— Beware of speaking:

An agile language creates many enemies.

— Find the best of men to work on them:

Rotten wood cannot be carved; walls filled with manure cannot be smoothed.

— Integrity:

A man survives because of his integrity. If he survives without it, it is pure luck.

— Honesty:

Raise honest people and place them above the dishonest, so that they can correct them.

— Loyalty, faith and justice:

Put loyalty and faith above all else and follow justice. This is how moral force is accumulated. When you love someone, you want them to live; when you hate someone, you want them to die. Now, to want to live and die at the same time is an example of incoherence.

— Virtue, knowledge, courage:

The wise do not suffer perplexity; the virtuous have no worries; the brave have no fear.

— Self-demand:

Demand much of yourselves, little of others, and you will avoid dissatisfaction.

—Seriousness in promises:

A promise made lightly is difficult to keep.

— Receptivity of opinions:

A gentleman does not approve a person for expressing a certain opinion, nor does he reject an opinion for being expressed by a certain person.

— Authority, not arrogance:

A gentleman shows authority, but not arrogance. A common man shows arrogance, but not authority.

— Ideal values for a human being:

A gentleman is governed by three principles that I am unable to follow: his humanity knows no anxiety; his wisdom has no doubts; his courage knows no fear.

— Autocorrect the errors:

No doubt it is a mistake not to correct a mistake.

— Do not live at the expense of your virtues:

A righteous man, a man who practices humanity, does not seek life at the expense of his humanity; on the contrary, there will be occasions when he will give his life to realize his humanity.

— Flexibility in conduct:

A gentleman has principles, but he is not rigid.

— Avoid bad company:

Three kinds of friends are beneficial; three kinds of friends are harmful. Friendship with upright, trustworthy and cultured people is beneficial. Friendship with crooked, flattering and false people is harmful.

— The five basic qualities of a human being:

Anyone who can expand the five practices around the world will increase humanity. - And what are these?: Courtesy, tolerance, good faith, diligence and generosity. Courtesy avoids insults; tolerance wins all hearts; good faith inspires trust in others; diligence ensures success; generosity confers authority over others.

— Misuse of virtue:

Those who make virtue their profession are the ruin of it.

— Avoid those who live on the lookout for the defects of others:

He hates those who stop at the defects of others. He hates subordinates who slander their superiors. He hates those whose courage is not moderated by civilized ways. He hates those who are impulsive and stubborn.

— Basic moral principles must not be violated:

Essential principles must not be transgressed. Secondary principles allow for some compromise.

— Justice and poverty:

Where there is justice there is no poverty.

— Firmness and impartiality:

The nobleman before nothing in the world adopts a closed attitude for or against. He adheres only to what is right. It is for everyone and it is impartial. Faced with what it does not understand, it suspends judgment. It is characterized by firmness of character, but not by obstinacy. It is treatable, but without intimacy. It is sure of itself, but not stubborn.

— Exemplarity in the governors:

If the prince is just, no one will be unjust; if the prince is kind, no one will be cruel.

— Virtuous attitude:

Much more excellent is the virtue of one who remains faithful to the practice of good, even if the country lacks laws and suffers poor administration.

— Know how to forgive:

Forgive all that nothing forgives itself.

— The human will above all:

You can take away a general's army, but not a man's will.

— More than punishments and sanctions to develop ethical values in the man to avoid the bad conducts:

Wouldn't it be more effective to make judgments unnecessary? Wouldn't it be more profitable to direct our efforts to the elimination of men's perverse inclinations?

— Defects and faults as a measure of a human being's values:

The defects and faults of men make known their true worth. If we carefully examine a man's faults, we will know whether his goodness is sincere or feigned.

— Trust and distrust at the same time:

When I began to deal with men, I listened to their words and trusted that their actions would conform to them. Now, in dealing with men, I hear their words and at the same time observe their actions.

— Maximum self-demand:

Be rigid with yourselves, but condescending to others. In this way you will be free from all envy and resentment.

— Shame, self-sacrifice, respect, consideration:

Whoever has never felt compassion towards others is not truly a man, neither can he be considered a true man who has never experienced feelings of shame and aversion; whoever does not possess the feelings of self-denial and respect cannot be considered a true man; whoever does not distinguish the true from the false, the just and the unjust, is not a man.

— Either good or evil, there is no middle ground:

In this world only two paths can be followed: the path of good or evil; there is no other possibility.

— Well-being and trust of the people under good governments:

The people distrust laws and administration; the people love good examples and good advice. With just laws and efficient administration, the revenue of the kingdom is increased; with good teachings and good examples, the heart of the subjects is conquered.

— Simplicity, honesty, justice:

The man of true distinction is simple, honest and a lover of justice and duty.

— Look at things from different perspectives:

It is in the cold of winter when you can see how green the pines and cypresses are.

— Get what you have earned with your effort:

No one should eat without having earned it.

— Respect for work:

Even the most humble professions are worthy of respect.

— Faithful to the performance of duty:

Perseverance in the right way and the constant practice of good works, when they have reached their maximum meadow of perfection, produce optimum results; in the same way, the faithful performance of duty will give rise to unlimited benefits, its cause being forces of a subtle and imperceptible nature.

— Eliminate your vices and defects before fighting against the vices and defects of others:

The most effective means of combating our vices and evil inclinations is not to combat the vices and evil inclinations of others before you have eliminated your own.

— Correction of vices:

Only he who commits a dishonourable act and does not correct himself can be qualified as "vicious".

— Do not propagate vices:

Whoever divulges the vicious actions of his fellow men builds his own ruin.

— Excessive wealth brings problems:

Some money avoids worries: much attracts them.

— Avoiding pomp and ostentation:

Pomp and ostentation serve very little for the conversion of peoples.

— Honesty before wealth:

Men aspire to riches and honours, but if it is not possible to obtain them by honest and upright means, they must renounce these goods.

Men flee poverty and insults, but if they cannot be avoided by honest and upright means, these evils must be accepted.

— Solidarity with the needy:
A worthy man must help the needy, but not increase the goods of the rich.

— Getting rich by bad means is a great evil.

Those who acquire wealth by violent and unjust means will likewise lose it by violent and unjust means.

— To be justly happy with what is necessary:

With rice to eat, water to drink and my arm folded by pillow I can be happy.

A happy man is a man who settles for little.

— Poor, but happy:

Satisfaction leads to happiness, even in poverty. And dissatisfaction leads to poverty, even in wealth.

— The end does not justify the means:

Happiness is not found at the top of the mountain, but in the way of climbing it.

— Against pride and frivolity:

Those who are prodigal in excess and give themselves to luxury, easily become proud.

— To obtain wealth only in an honest way:

I would be willing to exercise any trade if I could obtain great riches with it by honest means; if on the contrary, in order to enrich myself I had to use dishonest means, I would prefer to remain in poverty dedicating myself to my favourite activities.

— Wealth must not be an end:

If wealth were worthy of sleeplessness, I would even beat myself up, but not being so, I do as I please.

— Be ashamed of being rich when poverty abounds:

When order reigns in a country, it is a shame to be a poor and common man. When chaos reigns in a country, it is a shame to be rich and a civil servant.

IV.-CONFUCIUS APHORISMS ON ETHICS AND MORALS

A coward who casts fierce glances is — to put it bluntly — like a thief who climbs a wall.

A craftsman who wishes to do a good job must first sharpen his tools. In whatever country you settle, offer your services to the most virtuous of ministers and make friends with those knights who cultivate humanity.

A gentleman always resents his incompetence, not his anonymity.

A gentleman can be misinformed, but he cannot be seduced: he can be deceived, but he cannot be misled.

A gentleman does not approve a person for expressing a certain opinion, nor does he reject an opinion for being expressed by a certain person.

A gentleman eats without filling his belly; he chooses a dwelling without demanding comfort; he is diligent in his work and prudent in his speech; he seeks the company of the virtuous to correct his own conduct. Of such a man one can truly say that he has the desire to learn.

A gentleman has principles, but he is not rigid.

A gentleman is governed by three principles which I am unable to follow: his humanity knows no anxiety; his wisdom knows no doubt; his courage knows no fear.

A gentleman is tolerant and free; a common man is always full of anxiety and fear.

A gentleman pays attention in nine circumstances:

- When he looks, to see clearly.
- When he listens, to hear without confusion.
- In your expression, to be friendly.
- In your attitude, to be respectful.
- In your words, to be loyal.
- In your duties, to be responsible.
- When in doubt, to question.
- When you're angry, to reflect on the consequences.
- When he makes a profit, to consider whether it is fair.

A gentleman produces three kinds of impressions: if you look at him from afar, he seems severe. If you approach it, it is friendly. If you hear what he says, he is incisive.

A gentleman puts justice above all else. A knight who is brave, but not just, can become a rebel; a common man who is brave, but not just, can become a bandit. A gentleman seeks harmony, but not conformism. A common man seeks conformism, but not harmony.

A gentleman shows authority, but not arrogance. A common man shows arrogance, but not authority.

A gentleman worries about the possibility of disappearing from this world without having made a name for him.

A knight demands himself; a common man demands

A knight respects the wise and tolerates the mediocre; he praises the good and has compassion for the incapable. If I have great wisdom, who would I not tolerate? If I do not have great wisdom, people will avoid me; how then could I avoid them?

A long time ago I had a friend who practiced the following: competent, but willing to listen to the incompetent; talented, but willing to listen to those who lacked him; possessing him, he seemed not to have him; he accepted insults without being offended.

A man does not try to see himself in running water, but in calm water, because only what is calm in itself can give peace to others.

A man survives because of his integrity. If he survives without it, it is pure luck.

A man who does not meditate and act hastily will not be able to avoid great failures.

A man who values virtue more than good looks, who devotes all his energy to serving his father and mother, who is willing to give his life for his own sake Sovereign, and that in the relationship with his friends he is loyal to his word, though some may call him uneducated, I will continue to maintain that he is an educated man.

A man without virtue cannot endure adversity and joy for long. A good man rests in his humanity. A wise man knows how to use it.

A promise made lightly is difficult to keep.

A righteous man, a man who practices humanity, does not seek life at the expense of his humanity; on the contrary, there will be occasions when he will give his life to realize his humanity.

A single right word of the nobleman is enough for him to be considered understood about one thing, but it is also enough for him to make a single mistake to say that he knows nothing. Therefore, the nobleman must watch his words very carefully.

A virtue can never subsist in isolation; it must always be protected by other virtues.

A virtuous man always gives good advice; a man who gives good advice is not always virtuous. A good man is always brave; a brave man is not always good.

All beings participate in universal life, and do not harm one another. All the laws of the celestial bodies and those regulating the seasons are fulfilled simultaneously without interfering with each other. The forces of nature are manifested both by sliding a weak stream and by deploying enormous energies capable of transforming all beings, and this is precisely the greatness of heaven and earth.

All is forgiven to him who forgives nothing to himself.

An agile tongue creates many enemies.

An eminent position without nobility of character, worship without veneration, funerary practices without sincere pain: here are situations which I cannot bear.

And with what will you return the goodness? It is better to return justice for hatred, and kindness for kindness.

Anyone who can expand the five practices around the world will increase humanity. –

And what are these?: Courtesy, tolerance, good faith, diligence, and generosity. Courtesy avoids insults; tolerance wins all hearts; good faith inspires trust in others; diligence ensures success; generosity confers authority over others.

***Be** polite in private life; reverent in public life; loyal in personal relationships. Even among barbarians, don't stray from this attitude.*

Be rigid with yourselves, but condescending to others. In this way you will be free from all envy and resentment.

Better than the man who knows what is just is the man who loves what is just.

***Control** yourself even in your house; do not do, even in the most secret place, anything of which you may be ashamed.*

***Demand** much of yourselves, little of others, and you will avoid dissatisfaction.*

Driven by political manoeuvres and content with punishments, people become cunning and lose their shame. Driven by virtue and moderated by rites they develop a sense of shame and participation.

Essential principles must not be transgressed. Secondary principles allow for some compromise.

Even minor disciplines have their merits; but he who has a long journey before him fears the swamps, and that is why a gentleman does not go the less frequented ways.

Even the most humble professions are worthy of respect.

Find out a man's reasons for acting, observe how he acts, and examine where he finds peace. Is there anything else he could hide from us?

Firmness, resolution, simplicity and silence bring us closer to humanity.
For true friendship to develop, it is necessary to dispense with the superiority that can be bestowed by age, honours, riches, or power. The only motive that should incite us to friendship is the search for virtues and mutual perfection.

Forgive all that nothing forgives itself.

From the noblest man to the humblest, all have the duty to improve and correct their own being.

Give with your person to the people an example of virtue give with your person to the people an example of industriousness. Never stop doing so.

He cannot be qualified as noble who does not know the will of heaven; he cannot be seated on a firm foundation who does not know the laws of conveniences ("li"); he cannot know men who do not understand their words.

He hates those who stop at the defects of others. He hates subordinates who slander their superiors. He hates those whose courage is not moderated by civilized ways. He hates those who are impulsive and obstinate.

He is a man who, imposing himself on his self, submits to the "li" (customs), to the law of social conventions.

He who abstains from what he should not abstain from is better off abstaining from everything; he who treats with coldness those who should treat with tenderness will end up treating the whole world with coldness; those who advance hastily will also retreat with the same precipitation.

He who accepts to suffer will suffer half of his life; he who does not accept to suffer will suffer during his whole life.

He who desires for others what he would wish for himself, and does not do to his fellows what he would not have them do to him, possesses the righteousness of heart and fulfils the standard of moral conduct which man's own rational nature imposes upon him.

He who dominates his anger dominates his worst enemy.

He who is not faithful and sincere with his friends will never enjoy the trust of his superiors.

He, who knows how to keep a dignified posture even when he is among his friends, will get his closest friends to feel a great respect for him.

He who loves men strengthens men, for he himself desires to be strengthened; he helps men to achieve success for he himself desires to achieve success.

He who practices humanity is reluctant to speak.

He who speaks excessively and without sanity seldom puts into practice what he says.
The noble man never fears that his words will surpass his deeds.

He who, though surrounded by slander and deafened by criticism, remains calm, may be called perceptive. In fact, he could be called clairvoyant.

How could the words of admonition fail to get our feeling? The main thing, however, should really be to correct our behaviour. How could words of praise stop delighting us? However, the main thing should really be to understand their purpose. Some show delight, but no understanding, or nod, without changing their course. I really don't know what to do with them.

Human nature is neither good nor bad. According to this, the goodness or malice of men is something subsequent to human nature itself in its origin. If man possesses the capacity to act, it is necessary that he also possess a norm to direct his acts.

Humanity is more essential to people than water and fire. I have seen men lose their lives by surrendering to water or fire; I have never seen anyone lose their lives by surrendering to humanity.

I cannot expect to find a perfect man. I would be content to simply find a man of principle. It is difficult to have principles when Nothing pretends to be Something, Emptiness pretends to be Full and Poverty pretends to be Opulence

I do not understand how there can be men who act without knowing what they are doing.

I don't pay the slightest attention to the murmurings and criticisms of men.

I don't really know what to do with those who don't ask themselves, "What should I do before I take action?

I hate those who plagiarize by pretending to be cultured. I hate the arrogant who pretend to be brave. I hate maleficent who pretend to be frank.

I have never found it difficult to serve my superiors away from home and my elders at home, nor to bury the dead with due reverence or to moderate myself in wine.

I have never heard that a man who did not act uprightly could straighten others. Still less could he make others sincere if he observed hypocritical behaviour.

I have never met anyone who is really constant.

I have not found anyone who loves virtues with the same intensity with which one loves bodily beauty.

I have not known any man who always acted according to his principles. I do not do to others what I would not have them do to me.

I have not yet found any holy man; at most I have only managed to meet some wise man.
If a man has no humanity, what good are rites to him? If a man has no humanity, what is the use of music?

If a medicine does not alter the organism of the sick person, it will not produce a cure either.

If all the inhabitants of our village feel affection for a man, what should we think of him? This fact is not enough to pass judgment on this man.

If he only uses the work of his subjects to do what is reasonably necessary, who can experience resentment?

If he takes care of his outward appearance, if he is balanced and even-handed in all his acts, the whole people will respect him without fear; is not this authority free from despotism?

If his particular properties are neither too great nor too small, if he deals with matters which are neither too important nor too insignificant, if he keeps a certain distance from men without despising anyone, is not this dignity free from pride?

If I cannot find people who observe conventions to associate with them, I will be content with the mad and the pure. The madmen dare to do anything, while there are things that the pure ones will never do.

If I do not make sacrifices with all my heart, it is the same as if I did not make them.

If in all our businesses and companies we determine and plan in advance the stages of implementation, we will easily achieve success.

If the prince is just, no one will be unjust; if the prince is kind, no one will be cruel.

If the supreme good of man consisted in preserving life, he would do nothing but devote himself to discovering and practicing all that could prolong it. If the most fearsome evil of man were death, he would investigate and practice everything that could keep him away or prevent this evil. There are things that we love more than life, just as there are things more fearsome than death; this is a sentiment common to all men.

If the wise man observes a dismissive conduct, he will not inspire respect; if he limits himself to study, his knowledge will not be profound. You must always be sincere, faithful, and act in good faith.

If their best cultivate justice, the people will not dare to disobey. If their best cultivate good faith, the people will not dare to be a liar. In such a country, people would flock from everywhere with their babies wrapped around their backs.

If we determine in advance our standard of conduct in this life, at no time will our spirit be assailed by restlessness. If we know our duties beforehand, it will be easy for us to fulfil them.

If you get angry, think of the consequences.
If, before we start to speak, we determine and choose the words beforehand, our conversation will not be vacillating or ambiguous.

In archery, it does not matter whether the target is crossed or not, for archers may have different strength. That's the way it was once thought.

In the affairs of the world, a gentleman does not have a predetermined position: he adopts the position which is just.

In this world only two paths can be followed: the path of good or evil; there is no other possibility.

Inconsistency and impatience destroy the highest purposes.
Is goodness something unattainable? As long as he longs for goodness, it will be at hand.

It is as bad to go beyond the measure as it is not to reach it.

It is beautiful to live in the midst of humanity. It is

hardly wise to choose a place to live devoid of humanity:

It is easy to work for a gentleman, but it is not easy to please him. If you try to please him with immoral acts, he will not be pleased; but he never asks for anything that is beyond your capacity. It is not easy to work for a common man, but it is easy to please him. He tries to please him, even with an immoral course, and he will be pleased; but his demands know no bounds.

It is in the cold of winter when you can see how green the pines and cypresses are.
It is necessary for men to know evil in order to avoid it and to surrender to the practice of good.

It is necessary to act with rectitude without thinking of the consequences. We must not omit the fulfilment of our duties, nor carry them out ahead of time.

It is not your anonymity that should disturb you, but your incompetence.

It is possible to qualify as a superior man the one who first puts his ideas into practice, and then preaches to others what he already does.

It takes honest people and places them above the dishonest, so that they can correct them.

Man can extol the excellences of virtue, but virtue cannot bring prosperity and fame to man.

Man cannot fail to repent of his faults. If he once repents of not having repented of his faults, he will have no more cause for repentance.

Misfortunes, like fortune, only come when we have sought them with our acts.

Much more excellent is the virtue of one who remains faithful to the practice of good, even though the country lacks laws and suffers from poor administration.

My doctrine is all summarized in one thing: "tchung" (the means); or, perhaps, in one word: "shu" (equality, reciprocity, love of neighbour).

My zeal is as strong as anyone else's, but I have not yet managed to live nobly.

No doubt it's a mistake not to make amends.

No one should eat without having earned it.

Not cultivating moral strength, not exploring what I have learned, the inability to follow what I know is right, and to reform what is not good, these are all my concerns.

Not to foresee deception, not to suspect bad faith, but to be able to detect them immediately, that is certainly sagacity.

Nothing is more admirable in a noble man than to know how to accept and imitate the virtues of others.

Observe the wise to see if you possess their virtues.

Observe also the perverse ones to meditate in your interior if you are free from their defects.

Only a benevolent man can love and hate others.

Only he who commits a dishonourable act and does not correct himself can be called "vicious".

Our faults define us. It is from them that our qualities can be known.

Perseverance in the right way and the constant practice of good works, when they have reached their maximum meadow of perfection, produce optimum results; in the same way, the faithful fulfilment of duty will give rise to unlimited benefits, its cause being forces of a subtle and imperceptible nature.

Prudence advises not to be indignant when men deceive us, not to be sad when they are unfaithful. The prudent man always foresees these eventualities.

Reflect calmly before making any determination, never tire of doing good, and deal with each matter as appropriate.

Rotten wood cannot be carved; walls filled with manure cannot be smoothed.

Seek first of all the righteousness of our words, and then adjust our conduct to them. Always work in accordance with justice, to perfect ourselves every day in its realization. Inner anxieties come from

desiring the life of those we love, while we desire the death of those we could, since this is like desires at the same time the life and death of someone.
The perfect man does not place his greatest aspiration in riches.

Self-control rarely leads one to make mistakes.

Silence is the only friend who never betrays.

Speak with loyalty and good faith, act with dedication and respect, and even among the barbarians your conduct will be irreproachable. If you speak without loyalty and good faith, if you act without dedication and respect, your conduct will be unacceptable, even in your own hometown. Wherever you are, you must always keep this precept in mind; have it engraved on the yoke of your chariot, and only then will you be able to advance.

Superficial conversation ruins virtue. Small impatience ruins big plans.

Superficial talk and affected manners are seldom signs of kindness.

The best way to attain the virtues of justice and equity is to master the passions. He who allows himself to be dominated by passions is very difficult to act with justice and equity.

The common man is vain and proud, even when his position is not elevated. A man who is constant, patient, humble, and measured in speech is very close to perfection.

The courtesy that must preside over our daily actions is based principally on respect and understanding for all.

The defects and faults of men make known their true worth. If we look closely at a man's faults, we will come to know whether his goodness is sincere or feigned.

The error of a gentleman is like a solar or lunar eclipse. He makes a mistake, and everyone warns him; he corrects his mistake, and everyone admires him.

The gentleman considers the whole instead of the parts. The common man considers the parts instead of the whole.

The good man facilitates to others what he wishes to obtain for himself. The recipe for goodness consists simply in the ability to take one's aspirations as a guide.

The greatest defect of men is to worry about removing the tares from the fields of others, neglecting the cultivation of their own fields.

The kind man is measured in speaking. The noble man is the one who never feels regret or fear. Only he who, when he examines himself within, finds nothing bad, can be free from all sorrow and all fear.

The man of true distinction is simple, honest, and a lover of justice and duty.

The man who does not examine every day within himself what he should do, what he should imitate, what he should advise, and what he should reproach, will do nothing good in his life.

The man who does not meditate and act hastily will not be able to avoid great failures. You must always keep your head cool, your heart warm, and your hand outstretched.

The measure and the means are the culmination of human nature. The state in which neither hope, nor anger, nor sadness, nor joy is yet manifested, is called the medium.

The state in which they manifest themselves but get the right rhythm is called harmony.

The most effective means of combating our vices and bad inclinations is not to combat the vices and bad inclinations of others before we have eliminated our own.

The noble in practice allows himself to be guided by the "li" (customs).

The noble man preserves throughout his life the naivety and innocence of childhood.

The noble man, whatever the circumstances in which he finds himself, adapts to them so long as he always remains in the centre. As soon as he obtained a new virtue, he attached himself to it, perfected it within himself, and no longer abandoned it in all his life.

The noble promotes what is beautiful in man, the vile

what is ugly in man.

The nobleman before nothing in the world adopts a closed attitude for or against. He adheres only to what is right. It is for everyone and it is impartial. Faced with what it does not understand, it suspends judgment. It is characterized by firmness of character, but not by obstinacy. It is treatable, but without intimacy. He is sure of himself, but not stubborn.

The nobleman does not disregard his fellow men.

The nobleman does not give credit to words by the authority of the one who pronounces them; neither does he reject the truth even if it comes from an ignorant person.

The nobleman never expresses his opinion about things he does not understand. He seeks maximum precision in his words; this is the most important thing.

The only thing I want is not to fall into the need to boast about my virtues and my intelligence, and not to proclaim my good deeds.

The origin of all actions is found within our being. If, reflecting on our own acts, we discover that they are in conformity with our rational nature; we will experience the most intense satisfaction.

The people distrust laws and administration; the people love good examples and good counsel. With just laws and efficient administration, the revenue of the kingdom is increased; with good teachings and good examples, the heart of the subjects is conquered.

The people of old had three faults, which today cannot even be equalled. The eccentricity of the ancients was carefree, while today's eccentricity is licentious. The pride of the ancients was arrogant, while contemporary pride is grumpy. The naivety of the ancients was straight, while today's naivety is an imposture.

The prudent man is parochial in speaking but active in acting.

The right path or standard of moral conduct we must seek within ourselves. It is not a true norm of conduct that which is discovered outside of man, that is, that which does not derive directly from human nature itself.

The situation in which we find ourselves when joy, pleasure, anger, or sadness have not yet developed in our spirits is called the "centre. As soon as such passions begin to develop without exceeding a certain limit, we find ourselves in a state called "harmonious" or "balanced. The straight path of the universe is the centre, harmony is its universal and constant law.

The straight path is like a wide avenue; it is not difficult to find when one seeks it, but men do not strive to discover it.

The straight path is not followed. I know the cause of it. The learned men pass it; the ignorant do not reach it. Men of strong virtue go further; those of weak virtue do not.

The man of authentic virtue naturally perseveres in

the practice of the medium equally far from the extremes.

The street vendors of rumours are people who have abandoned virtue.

The superior man neither argues nor fights with anyone. He only argues when it is necessary to clarify something, but even then he gives first place to his defeated antagonist and goes up to the room with him; once the discussion is over, he drinks with his opponent as a sign of peace. These are the only arguments of the superior man.

The trials of a good man bear his fruit: this is undoubtedly goodness.

The vices come as passengers, visit us as guests and stay as masters.

The vicious men try to conceal their faults with appearances of honesty.

The wise do not suffer perplexity; the virtuous have no worries; the brave have no fear.

The wise find joy in the water, the kind find joy in the mountains. The wise are active, the kind are gentle. The wise are joyful, the kind live long.

They put loyalty and faith above all else, and justice follows. This is how moral force is accumulated. When you love someone, you want them to live; when you hate someone, you want them to die. Now, to want someone to live and die at the same time is an example of incoherence.

Those who are impetuous, but not sincere, those who are ignorant, and also reckless; those who are naive, but not trustworthy, are beyond my comprehension.

Those who control their actions at all times rarely deviate from the right path.

Those who make virtue their profession are the ruin of it.

Three kinds of friends are beneficial; three kinds of friends are harmful. Friendship with righteous, trustworthy and cultured people is beneficial. Friendship with crooked, flattering, and false people is harmful.

To be strict with oneself and restrained with others is acceptable. To be restrained with oneself and restrained with others would be too much laxity.

To desire only the riches necessary for the practice of the virtues proper to his dignity, can this be called "greed"?

To do all that is for the common good; is this not the best form of generosity?

To enjoy prestige and consideration is one of the things men aspire to most ardently.

To have sufficient self-control to judge others by comparison with ourselves, and to act in relation to them as we would wish them to do with us, this is what can be called the doctrine of humanity; there is nothing beyond this.

To know something is not as good as to love it; to love something is not as good as to enjoy it.

To know what is right and not to practice it is cowardice.

To Love All

To make our intentions right and sincere we must act in accordance with our natural inclinations.

To possess capacity and talents, and to accept the opinion of those who lack them; to have much and to accept the opinion of those who have nothing; to be rich and to behave as if they were poor; to be full and to appear empty and devoid of everything; to let oneself be offended without showing resentment; at one time I had a friend who behaved in this way in life.

Trapped by poverty, a brave man may rebel. If you push him too far, a man without morals can also rebel.

Truth cannot depart from human nature. If what we consider truth departs from human nature, then it cannot be truth.

Unfortunately, I have never seen a man able to see his own faults and to expose them before the court of his heart.

We must not be afflicted that men do not know you. The unfortunate thing is that you are not worthy to be known by men.

What does goodness consist of? To love all men.

What is death? If we do not yet know what life is, how can it disturb us to know the essence of death?

What is done is done; everything belongs to the past, and there is no point in arguing.

What is the most important thing to achieve correct behaviour? Be sincere at all times and always keep the word given. Try to make even the smallest gesture reflect inner dignity, and not commit any amazing action. If you do so, your conduct will be admired everywhere, even among barbarian peoples. On the contrary, if you are not sincere, if you break your promises, if your gestures are not worthy or your actions are dishonourable, your conduct will be despised both in a city of 10,000 families and in a village of 35 neighbours.

What you disapprove of your superiors, do not practice with your subordinates, not what you disapprove of your subordinates you must practice with your superiors. What you disapprove of those who have gone before you, do not practice with those who follow you, and what you disapprove of those who follow you, do not do to those who are before you.

Whatever you do belongs to you; I alone must answer for my own acts.

When a man is rejected by all, one should investigate.

When everyone likes someone, one should investigate.

When he faces danger, a knight is prepared to give his life; the prospect of profit does not make him forget what is just; when he celebrates sacrifices, he does so with pity; when he is in mourning, he expresses his sorrow. What more can one desire?

When heaven sends us calamities, we can overcome them; when we have sought them ourselves, we will succumb to them.

When I began to deal with men, I listened to their words and was confident that their actions would conform to them. Now, in dealing with men, I hear their words and at the same time I observe their actions.

When man is near death, his words are sincere and truthful.

When many people stay together for a whole day, not everything that is said is fair and equitable. It is very frequent to talk about vulgar things and that foolish conversations abound.

When one does not yet know what life is, how can one know what death is?

When one examines one's interiority and finds that there is nothing wrong with it, why should it be sad, what should one fear?

When one has not yet attained perfection in the service of men, how is it possible that he is worthy to serve the spirits?

When one is in the service of a lord, pettiness attracts

misfortune; in friendly relations, pettiness attracts distancing.

When one seeks to realize humanity, there is no place for evil.

When the centre and harmony have reached their highest degree of perfection, peace and order reign in heaven and on earth, and all beings reach their full development.

When the crowd despises someone, you must objectively examine his conduct before you give your opinion. Even when the crowd cheers for someone, it is necessary to look at his works impartially before approving them.

When the heart is agitated, it is offered routinely. Therefore, only the sage is able to exhaust the meaning of the offering. Nothing is more admirable in a noble man than knowing how to accept and imitate the virtues of others.

When the soul is agitated by anger, it lacks this fortress; when the soul is inhibited by fear, it lacks this fortress; when the soul is intoxicated by pleasure, it cannot stay strong; when the soul is overwhelmed by pain, it cannot reach this fortress either. When our spirit has been troubled for any reason, we look and do not see, hear and do not hear, eat and do not taste.

When you see an honest man, try to imitate him. When you see a man who is not honest, examine yourselves (examine whether you have the same defects).

When you wait for a gentleman, you have to avoid

three mistakes. It is imprudent to speak before being invited to do so. It is excessive reserve not to speak when invited to do so. It is blindness to speak without observing the gentleman's expression.

Where there is justice there is no poverty.

Whoever discloses the vicious actions of his fellow men builds his own ruin.

Whoever has never felt compassion towards others is not truly a man, neither can he be considered a true man who has never experienced feelings of shame and aversion; whoever does not possess the feelings of self-denial and respect cannot be considered a true man; whoever does not distinguish the true from the false, the just and the unjust, is not a man.

Whoever loves men is loved by them; whoever respects them is, in turn, respected. Let us suppose that having behaved discourteously or rudely towards us; if we are prudent, the first thing we must ask ourselves is whether we have previously committed any discourtesy towards such a person or whether we have been unfair to him; his attitude towards us must have some foundation. If we come to the conclusion that we have not done any injustice to such a person, but have always shown ourselves to him kind and courteous, we must continue to analyze the possible causes of discourteous or rude attitude. If we are prudent, we must reflect whether we have committed the slightest impropriety in our conduct. Assuming that we have not committed any wrongdoing either, then the discourtesy or rudeness of the offended person is totally unfounded, and the prudent man, faced with such a situation, must conclude: "This man is nothing more than an extravagant and a fool; he is nothing different from a beast, in which case, why should I care about the attitude or acts of a beast?".

Whoever shows cordiality and demanding attention deserves to be called a gentleman: Demanding attention to friends and cordiality to brothers.

Words in themselves are innocuous, but their consequences can be disastrous if they are derogatory.

Would it not be more effective to make judgments unnecessary? Would it not be more profitable to direct our efforts to the elimination of the perverse inclinations of men?

You ask me why I buy rice and flowers? I buy rice to live and flowers to have something to live for.

You can take away a general's army, but not a man's will.

APPENDIX

Some concepts used in this essay deserve to be briefly elaborated upon.

ETHICS: A set of moral norms that govern the conduct of people in any sphere of life. It is part of the philosophy that deals with the good and the foundation of its values. Ethics is different from morality, because morality is based on obedience to cultural, hierarchical or religious norms, customs and precepts or commandments, while ethics seeks to support the way of living by human thought. In philosophy, ethics is not limited to morality, which is generally understood as custom or habit, but seeks the theoretical foundation to find the best way to live, the search for the best lifestyle.

MORAL: Relative to people's actions, from the point of view of their actions in relation to good or evil and in function of their individual and, above all, collective life. Based on understanding or consciousness, and not senses. Prove, moral certainty. It concerns the internal forum or human respect, and not the legal order. Doctrine of human action that seeks to regulate individual and collective behaviour in relation to good and evil and the duties they imply. Set of faculties of the spirit, as opposed to the physical or material. State of mind: individual or collective. Encourage to face something. In activities that involve confrontation or intense effort, confidence in success.

VALUES: In a generic sense, values are the properties, qualities or characteristics of an action, a person, or an object considered typically positive, or of great importance. Values that are influenced or determined by a particular society and culture are often referred to as social values and cultural values. Those that are considered from the point of view of Ethics and Morality are ethical values and moral values. Ethical values are behavioural guidelines that regulate behaviour, have a universal character and are acquired during the individual development of each person. Moral values are those that are transmitted by society, in some cases are determined by a religious doctrine and can change over time.

PERSONALITY: It is the individual difference that distinguishes one person from another. As such, personality is the term that describes and allows giving a theoretical explanation of the set of peculiarities possessed by an individual that characterizes him and differentiates him from others. The concept of personality comes from the term "person".

SOCIETY: It is a group of beings that live in an organized way. The word comes from the Latin "societas", which means friendly association with others. The concept of society presupposes the coexistence and joint activity of man, consciously organized or ordered, and implies a certain degree of communication and cooperation. It is the general objective of the study of the ancient sciences of the state, today called social sciences.

POLITICS: Art, doctrine or opinion regarding the government of the States, activity of those who manage or aspire to manage public affairs, activity of the citizen when he intervenes in public affairs with his opinion, with his vote, or in any other way, courtesy and good behaviour, the art or layout by which a matter is conducted or the means used to achieve a particular end; orientations or directives that govern the action of a person or entity in a given matter or field.

GLOBALIZATION: It is a historical process of world integration in the political, economic, social, cultural and technological spheres, which has turned the world into an increasingly interconnected place, into a global village. As such, globalization was the result of the consolidation of capitalism, of major technological advances (technological revolution) and of the need to expand the world trade flow.

PRODUCTIVE FORCES: Marxist term used to designate the set of means of production and the men who use them to produce material goods. Within the means of production, the means of work constitute the material and technical basis of society. The productive forces express the relationship that exists between man and the objects and forces of nature, the degree to which nature dominates them, thus defining the level of development of humanity in a particular epoch. The productive forces are constantly and rapidly developing and perfecting themselves, which must also determine changes in the production relations in force in society which, if they are not fulfilled, create deep tensions and contradictions that need to be resolve

PRODUCTION RELATIONS: Marxist term that refers to the relations established between men in the production process and that at the same time define the modes of production: slave, feudal, capitalist, and socialist, among others. Within them are the relations of property, labour, socioeconomic dependence, etc. also the form of distribution of production and wealth. They are conditioned and closely related to the productive forces.

ZHOU DYNASTY. The Zhou dynasty was the third of the ancient Chinese dynasty it lasted for more than seven centuries, from 1027 to 221 B.C. This dynasty, key in Chinese culture, was founded by the Ji family and its capital was in Hao (near the present city of Xian). In Western historiography, the Zhou period is often described as feudal due to the decentralized character of their mandate comparable to the medieval system of Europe. When the royal lineage collapsed, the power of the Zhou gradually diminished: the fragmentation of the kingdom accelerated and in the end the emperors officially reigned, but power actually resided in the hands of the powerful nobility. Towards the end of the Zhou Dynasty, the nobles did not even bother to thank the Ji family symbolically and declared themselves kings. They wanted to be the kings of kings. Finally, the dynasty was destroyed by the unification of Qin Shi Huang from China in the year 221 BC.

CONFUCIANISM: Doctrine whose purpose is to find harmony between man and society. Its foundations can be found in the so-called "Four Classical Books of Confucius" written later by his disciples and followers.

ANALECTS OF CONFUCIUS. The term alludes to a collection of selected literary fragments by one or more authors. In the subject we are studying, they constitute the truest text of Confucian doctrines, a series of short and coherent statements, dialogues and anecdotes. They were compiled by the following first generations of disciples of Confucius. They do not have a pre-established order or homogeneity.

DEFINITION OF OTHER TERMS.

According to the doctrine of Confucius it is necessary to define the terms way, rite and knights.

THE WAY: Refers to justice, the correct action of a State.

RITO: It is understood in the doctrines of Confucius as tradition, ethical customs, and moral.

KNIGHTS: Men formed ethically and socially, independently of their social origin. It differs completely from the concept of feudal knight, noble title obtained in a hereditary way.

ANNEX I.

CONFUCIUS

THE FOUR CLASSICAL BOOKS.

First Classical Book (Ta-Hio or Great Science). It is attributed to the grandson of Kung-Tse (Confucius) and deals, in essence, with the knowledge of the human being in his age of maturity.

Second Classic Book (Chung-Yung or Doctrine of the Middle). Its content focuses on the norms or rules that govern the conduct of the human being, the ethics and exemplarity of the rulers and the justice related to them.

Third Classic Book (Mon-Yu or Philosophical Comments). Generally known as "Analects" where the essential of the doctrine of Kung-Tse is summarized in a dialogued form.

Fourth Classical Book (Meng-Tse or Book of Mencio) written by his most prominent follower, who lived between 371 and 289 BC.

SUMMARIZED VERSION OF THE FOUR CLASSIC CONFUCIUS BOOKS

FIRST CLASSIC BOOK (TA-HIO OR GREAT SCIENCE)*

It is necessary to know the end towards which we must direct our actions. As soon as we know the essence of all things, we will have reached the state of perfection that we had set for ourselves.

From the noblest to the humblest man, everyone has the duty to improve and correct his own being.

Would it not be more effective to make judgments unnecessary? Would it not be more profitable to direct our efforts to the elimination of the perverse inclinations of men?

To make our intentions right and sincere, we must act in accordance with our natural inclinations.

When the soul is agitated by anger, it lacks this fortress; when the soul is inhibited by fear, it lacks this fortress; when the soul is intoxicated by pleasure, it cannot stand strong; when the soul is overwhelmed by pain, it cannot reach this fortress either. When our spirit has been troubled for any reason, we look and do not see, hear and do not hear, eat and do not taste.

Rarely do men recognize the defects of those whom they love, and they are not accustomed either to valuing the virtues of those whom they hate.

What you disapprove of your superiors, you do not practice with your subordinates, no what you disapprove of your subordinates you must practice with your superiors. What you disapprove of those who have preceded you, do not practice with those who follow you, and what you disapprove of those who follow you, do not practice with those who are in front of you.

Not giving importance to the principal, that is, to the cultivation of intelligence and character, and seeking only the accessory, that is, wealth, can only give rise to the perversion of the feelings of the people, who will also value only wealth and give themselves unchecked to theft and plunder.

If the prince uses public rents to increase his personal wealth, the people will imitate this example and give free rein to their most perverse inclinations; if, on the contrary, the prince uses public rents for the good of the people, the people will be submissive to him and will be kept in order.

If the prince or magistrates promulgate unjust laws or decrees, the people will not comply with them and will oppose their execution by violent and unjust means. Those who acquire wealth by violent and unjust means shall likewise lose it by violent and unjust means.

There is only one way to increase the public revenues of a kingdom: let there be many who produce and few who dissipate, let there be much work and let there be moderation in spending. If all the people do so, the profits will always be sufficient.

*This text is also known as the book of Great Knowledge, Great Science and Great Learning. The main text is attributed to Confucius, to which are added about ten chapters of commentaries attributed to Zengzi. In short, it refers to the balance, harmony and moral perfection of the individual: rest, reflection, peace of mind, study, self-learning, the desire to overcome oneself through individual effort, independently of the social status of the individual and the establishment of priorities, among other aspects. The elements of knowledge are not isolated and the success or failure of one of them will affect the others.

SECOND CLASSIC BOOK (CHUNG-YUNG OR THE DOCTRINE OF THE MEDIUM).**

The situation in which we find ourselves, when joy, pleasure, anger or sadness have not yet developed in our spirits, is called the "centre". As soon as such passions begin to develop without exceeding a certain limit, we find ourselves in a state called "harmonious" or "balanced. The straight path of the universe is the centre; harmony is its universal and constant law.

When the centre and harmony have reached their highest degree of perfection, peace and order reign in heaven and on earth, and all beings reach their full development.

The noble man, whatever the circumstances in which he finds himself, adapts to them so that he always remains in the centre. As soon as he obtained a new virtue, he attached himself to it, perfected it within himself, and no longer abandoned it in all his life.

Much more excellent is the virtue of one who remains faithful to the practice of good, even though the country lacks laws and suffers poor administration.

The right path, or standard of moral conduct, must be sought within us.

It is not a true standard of conduct that which is

discovered outside of man, that is, that which does not derive directly from human nature itself.

He who desires for others what he would wish for himself, and does not do to his fellow men what he would not have them do to him, possesses the righteousness of heart and fulfils the standard of moral conduct which his own rational nature imposes on man.

Perseverance in the right path and the constant practice of good works, when they have reached their maximum meadow of perfection, produce excellent results; in the same way, the faithful fulfilment of duty will give rise to unlimited benefits, its cause being forces of a subtle and imperceptible nature.

There are five fundamental and common duties and three faculties to practice them.

These duties refer to the following five relationships: the relationships that must exist between the prince and his subjects, between the father and his children, between husband and wife, between older and younger brothers, and between friends. Righteous behaviour in these five relationships constitutes the principal duty common to all men.

For the good government of the realms the observance of nine universal rules is necessary: the mastery and perfection of oneself, respect for the wise, love for the family, consideration for ministers as the principal officials of the kingdom, perfect harmony with all subordinate officials and magistrates, cordial relations with all subjects, acceptance of the advice and guidance of sages and artists with whom the ruler must always surround himself, courtesy to passers-by and foreigners, and honourable and benign treatment of vassals.

If, before we begin to speak, we determine and choose the words beforehand, our conversation will not be hesitant or ambiguous. If in all our businesses and companies we determine and plan in advance the stages of action, we will easily achieve success. If we determine our standard of conduct in this life sufficiently in advance, at no time will our spirit be assailed by restlessness? If we know our duties beforehand, it will be easy for us to fulfil them.

He who is not faithful and sincere with his friends will never enjoy the confidence of his superiors.

When the prudent man is elevated to sovereign dignity, he does not take pride or pride in it; if his position is humble, he does not rebel against the rich and powerful.

When the kingdom is administered justly and equitably, his word will suffice to confer upon it the dignity it deserves; when the kingdom is misgoverned, and riots and seditions occur, his silence will suffice to save his person.

All beings participate in universal life, and do not harm one another. All the laws of the heavenly bodies and those regulating the seasons are fulfilled simultaneously without interfering with each other. The forces of nature are manifested both by sliding a weak stream and by deploying enormous energies capable of transforming all beings, and this is precisely the greatness of heaven and earth.

The sage pretends that his virtuous actions pass unnoticed by men, but day by day they are revealed with greater radiance; on the contrary, the inferior man ostentatiously performs virtuous actions, but they vanish quickly. The conduct of a wise man is like water: he lacks taste, but all are pleased; he lacks colour, but he is beautiful and captivating; he lacks form, but he adapts himself with simplicity and order to the most varied figures.

Control yourself even in your own house; do not do, even in the most secret place, anything of which you may be ashamed.

Without offering material goods, the wise earn the love of all; without being cruel and headlong, he is feared by the people more than axes and spears.

Pomp and ostentation are of little use in the conversion of peoples.

**Related to the doctrine of the centre or middle: The centre is the state in which we find ourselves when we have not achieved joy, pleasure, anger or sadness, without exceeding certain limits at that time we will have reached a harmonious state and balance, In the moment that the centre and harmony have achieved their highest degree of perfection is in which peace and order reign on earth and in heaven. The noble man tries to remain in the centre regardless of circumstances, so the right path or perfect moral conduct must be achieved within us.

THIRD CLASSIC BOOK (LUN-YU OR PHILOSOPHICAL COMMENTARIES). ANALECTS. ***

If the wise man observes a dismissive behaviour, he will not inspire respect; if he limits himself to study, his knowledge will not be deep. You must always be sincere, faithful, and act in good faith. Do not befriend people of virtue or knowledge inferior to yours. If you have a defect, try to correct it.

The courtesy that should preside over our daily actions is based mainly on respect and understanding for all.

A man can be called a "superior man" if he first puts his ideas into practice, and then preaches to others what he already does.

True science consists in knowing that one knows what one really knows, and that one ignores what one really ignores. This is what true wisdom is all about.

Learn to listen without rest to dispel your doubts; look at your words, so that nothing you say is superfluous; only in this way will you be able to avoid all error. Observe everything, to prevent the damage that could be caused by insufficient information. Control your actions so that you do not have to regret them often. As soon as you have succeeded in making your words normally straight, and you should not frequently regret your actions, you will be worthy of the office you occupy.

To know what is right and not to practice it is cowardice.

The superior man does not argue or quarrel with anyone. He only argues when it is necessary to clarify something, but even then he gives first place to his defeated antagonist and goes up to the room with him; once the discussion is over, he drinks with his opponent as a sign of peace. These are the only discussions of the superior man.

Men long for riches and honours, but if it is not possible to obtain them by honest and upright means, they must renounce these goods. Men flee poverty and insults, but if they cannot be avoided by honest and upright means, these evils must be accepted.

The defects and faults of men make known their true worth. If we examine attentively the faults of a man, we will come to know whether his goodness is sincere or feigned.

Observe the sages to see if you possess their virtues. Observe also the perverse ones to meditate in your interior if you are free of their defects.

Those who control their actions at all times rarely deviate from the straight path.

A virtue can never survive in isolation; it must always be protected by other virtues.

A prudent man is parochial in speaking but active in acting.

When I began to deal with men, I listened to their words and trusted that their actions would conform to them. Now, in dealing with men, I hear their words and, at the same time, I observe their actions.

I have not known a man who always acted according to his principles. I do not do to others what I would not have them do to me.

He who knows how to keep a dignified posture even when he is among his friends, will get his closest friends to feel a great respect for him.

My only ambition and desire is not to fall into the need to boast of my virtues and intelligence, and not to proclaim my good deeds.

A worthy man should help the needy, but not increase the goods of the rich.

It is better to love the truth than to coldly know it; it is better to indulge in the practice of truth than to simply love it.

I would be willing to exercise any office if with it I could obtain great wealth by honest means; if, on the contrary, in order to enrich myself I had to use dishonest means, I would prefer to remain in poverty dedicating myself to my favourite activities
I have not yet found any holy man; at most I have only managed to know some wise man. I do not understand how men can act without knowing what they are doing.

Those who are lavish in excess and indulge in luxury easily become proud.

When man is near death, his words are sincere and truthful.

It is possible to get the people to follow the good man, but they can never be forced to understand him.

In general, men love bodily beauty more than virtue.

When one has not yet attained perfection in the service of men, how is it possible that he is worthy to serve the spirits?

What is death? If we do not yet know what life is, how can it disturb us to know the essence of death?

It is as bad to go beyond the measure as it is not to reach it.

In public, always behave as if you were in front of a very distinguished person; when you have to give some order to the people, show the same respect and dignity as if you were offering the great sacrifice. Do not want for others what you do not want for yourself.

The kind man is measured in speaking. The noble man is the one who never feels regret or fear. Only he who, when he examines himself within himself, finds nothing bad, can be free from all sorrow and fear.

It is utterly impossible to govern a people if it has lost confidence in its rulers.

Seek first of all the righteousness of our words, and then adjust our conduct to them. Always work in accordance with justice, to perfect ourselves every day in its realization. Inner anxieties come from desiring the life of those you love, while you desire the death of those you could, because it like desires at the same time the life and death of someone. The perfect man does not put his greatest aspiration into riches.

Reflect calmly before making any determination, never tire of doing good, and deal with each matter as appropriate.

The first thing the chief must see is that his conduct is simple, upright, and just at all times; that he always takes into account the advice of other men, that he always controls his own acts, and that he should never command despotically.

The most effective means of combating our vices and bad inclinations is not to combat the vices and bad inclinations of others before having eliminated one's own.

In what does goodness consist? To love all men. What does science consist of? In knowing men. The nobleman never expresses his opinion about things he does not understand. He seeks maximum precision in his words; this is the most important thing.

If he who governs is not just, even if he commands that justice be practiced, he will not be obeyed.

When the people are so numerous, what can be done for their good? Make them rich and happy. And when he is rich, what more can be done for him? Educate him.

He who control himself and for the good will have no difficulty in governing effectively. Those who do not know how to govern themselves will find it impossible to order the conduct of other men.

What is the essence of good government? Do not resolve matters hastily and do not seek your own profit.

If all the inhabitants of our village have affection for a man, what should we think of him? This fact is not enough to pass judgment upon such a man.

The common man is vain and proud, even when his position is not high. The man who is constant, patient, humble, and measured in speech is very near to perfection.

Punishments should be imposed when appropriate. Fidelity is not contrary to just correction.

He who speaks excessively and without sanity rarely puts into practice what he says. The noble man never fears that his words will surpass his deeds.

It should not afflict us that men do not know you. The unfortunate thing is that you are not worthy to be known by men.

Prudence advises not to be indignant when men deceive us, not to be sad when they are unfaithful. The prudent man always foresees these eventualities.

He who, as a child, has not respected his brothers or his parents, has not done anything useful in old age, and when old age comes he has not died, is a despicable man.

What is the most important to achieve correct behaviour? Be sincere at all times and always keep the word given. See that even the smallest gesture reflects inner dignity, and do not commit any astonishing action. If you do so, your conduct will be admired everywhere, even among barbarian peoples. On the contrary, if you are not sincere, if you break your promises, if your gestures are not worthy or your actions are dishonourable, your conduct will be despised both in a city of 10,000 families and in a village of 35 neighbours.

The man who does not meditate and act with haste will not be able to avoid great failures.

I have not found anyone who loves virtues with the same intensity with which one loves bodily beauty.

Be rigid with yourselves, but condescending to others. In this way you will be free from all envy and resentment.

The man who does not examine every day within himself what he must do, what he must imitate, what he must advise, and what he must reproach, will do nothing good in his life.

When many people remain together for a whole day, not all that is said is just and equitable. It is very frequent to talk about vulgar things and that foolish conversations abound.

A nobleman does not give credit to words by the authority of the one who pronounces them; neither does he reject the truth even if it comes from an ignorant person.

Inconsistency and impatience destroy the highest purposes.

When the crowd despises someone, you must objectively examine his conduct before giving your opinion. Also when the multitude acclaims someone, it is necessary to contemplate with impartiality their works before approving them.

Man can extol the excellences of virtue, but virtue cannot bring prosperity and fame to man.

Only he who commits a dishonourable act and is not corrected can be called "vicious.

The nobleman only seeks the truth and does not cling with blind obstinacy to his criterion.

Transmit culture to the whole world, without distinction of race or category.

Words must faithfully express our thought.

The ministers of a virtuous prince must avoid three faults: petulance, which consists in speaking when no one has asked them for their opinion; shyness, which consists in not daring to express their opinion when invited to do so; and imprudence, which consists in speaking without first having observed the prince's state of mind.

Only the men of deep intelligence and the fools of the most obtuse mind remain invariable.

If a hen is killed, why use a knife, which is used to kill oxen?

If you respect your own person and all our fellow men, no one can despise you; if you are generous, you will earn the affection of the people; if you are sincere, no one will distrust you; if all your actions bring you closer to good, your merit will be great; love for men is the best weapon to govern effectively.

Even the humblest professions are worthy of respect.

A "lover of study" is one who each day acquires new knowledge, and each month retains what he has learned.

Do not be ashamed to ask questions to resolve your doubts, and meditate on the answers that have been given to you.

Vicious men try to disguise their faults with appearances of honesty.

A single right word of the nobleman is enough to be considered understood about a thing, but it is also enough that he makes only one mistake to say that he knows nothing. Therefore, the nobleman must watch his words very carefully.

The good ruler must be generous without falling into prodigality; he must collect sufficient taxes to lead a dignified life, without falling into greed; his bearing must be dignified and grave, without being led by vain ostentation; he must have authority, without his command being despotic; he must cautiously demand the collaboration of the people in public works, so as not to arouse their resentment.

To do everything for the common good is this not the best form of generosity?

To desire only the riches necessary for the practice of the virtues proper to his dignity, can this be called "covetousness"? If his particular properties are neither too great nor too small, if he deals with matters that are neither too important nor too insignificant, if he keeps a certain distance from men without despising anyone, is not this dignity free from pride? If he takes care of his outward appearance, if he is balanced and even-handed in all his acts, the whole people will respect him without fear; is not this authority free from despotism? If it only uses the work of the subjects to do what is reasonably necessary, who can experience resentment?

The four vices concerning government are as follows: not to instruct the people and to hide the truth, which is called "tyranny"; to demand perfect conduct from all citizens without first informing them of their obligations, which is called "oppression"; not to be in a hurry to give orders and then to expect them to be carried out on the spot, which is a grave injustice; always to seek one's own profit, which is called "selfishness".

***The Analects constitute a series of conversations or dialogues of Confucius with his disciples and constitute a relevant aspect of Confucianism as a doctrine. In them the contents are arranged independently without following a specific order. Therefore, it is to be assumed that the book was written by several of his disciples or followers. It should be noted that Analects have had a significant influence on the ethics and philosophy of Asian peoples, especially in China, because they contain the fundamental elements of Confucianism: rectitude, decency, loyalty and filial love.

FOURTH CLASSIC BOOK (MENG-TSE OR MENCIUS BOOK). ****

If profit or profit takes precedence over justice, the subjects will never be satisfied and the prince will be in constant danger.

If men with grey hair can cover themselves with silk garments and eat meat, if the young men with black hair cease to suffer hunger and cold, the life of the kingdom will be prosperous. There has not been a single prince who, doing so, has failed to gain authority over his people.

If a king does not govern with righteousness, that is, if he does not fill his people with benefits, it is because he does not want to, and not because he cannot.

If a prince is saddened by the misfortunes of his people, the subjects will also feel sorrow for the sorrows of their prince. If the prince rejoices in the happiness of his people, and makes his own the hardships of his subjects, he will have no difficulty in his government.

If you madly love riches, you must do nothing but share them with the people.

What the rulers do is then imitated by the people. You cannot, therefore, now accuse or condemn the people for their conduct, for they have imitated what they had learned from their prince.

The nobleman who seeks to found a dynasty does not aspire to be elevated to Imperial dignity, but merely prepares the way for his descendants; if the will of heaven is propitious to him, he himself will be elevated to supreme dignity.

Wisdom and prudence are of no use unless there is a propitious occasion; good ploughs can do nothing by themselves, unless there is a propitious season.

It is necessary to act uprightly without thinking of the consequences. We must not omit the fulfilment of our duties, nor carry them out ahead of time.

Whoever tries to subdue men by the force of arms will not achieve the submission of their hearts; therefore, violence is never enough to dominate men. He who conquers men by virtue makes them all submit to it without reserve and with a cheerful heart.

Misfortunes, like fortune, only come when we have sought them with our actions.

When heaven sends us calamities, we can overcome them; when we have sought them ourselves, we will succumb to them.

He who has never felt compassion for others is not truly a man, nor can he be considered a true man who has never experienced feelings of shame and aversion; he who does not possess the feelings of self-denial and respect cannot be considered a true man; he who does not distinguish the true from the false, the just and the unjust, is not a man.

Nothing is more admirable in a noble man than to

know how to accept and imitate the virtues of others.

Whatever you do belongs to you; I alone must answer for my own acts.

Neither the fortifications that are built, nor the natural obstacles represented by mountains and rivers, nor the abundance of weapons are sufficient for the defence of a kingdom. The best defence of a kingdom consists in the determined will of its inhabitants, which is conquered by a humanitarian and just government.

Whoever holds a public office and is unable to fulfil his obligations must resign.

If a medicine does not alter the organism of the sick person, it will not produce a cure either.

He who thinks only of accumulating wealth cannot be good; he who thinks only of practicing good cannot be rich.

If the teachers clearly teach the duties to all the citizens of the kingdom, they will live among themselves in harmony and harmony.

Generosity consists in distributing wealth among the needy; righteousness consists in seeking the way of good to the erring; goodness is the virtue that the emperor must possess in order to gain the affection of all his subjects.

In this world only two paths can be followed: the path of good or evil; there is no other possibility.

The small kingdoms imitate the powerful, but they are ashamed to take orders from them and do not want to obey them.

The kingdoms perish because of their internal decomposition before the other kingdoms attack them.

You look for the right path in the distance and have it with you. You believe that good consists in the accomplishment of difficult things, when it is nothing more than the righteous accomplishment of easy things.

When wars are waged to conquer new territories, the fields will be covered by the bodies of the victims.

No greater evil can be thought of than the loss of mutual affection and affection between parents and children.

There are men who are known as great creators because no one has ever refuted their flimsy arguments. One of the main faults of men is that of pretending to be a model for others.

The rules of conduct are immutable; all the Saints have acted in accordance with their principles.

When the prince begins to punish his officials without having committed any crime, prudent ministers hasten to leave the kingdom.

If the prince is just, no one will be unjust; if the prince is kind, no one will be cruel.

It is necessary for men to know evil in order to

avoid it and to give themselves to the practice of good.

He who divulges the vicious actions of his fellow men builds his own ruin.

The noble man preserves throughout his life the ingenuity and innocence of childhood.

The wise man, as soon as he has reached a virtue, clings strongly to it and never loses it; as soon as he has perfected to the maximum the acquired virtue, he keeps it carefully within himself as an inexhaustible source of energy.

Words themselves are innocuous, but their consequences can be disastrous if they are derogatory.

He who loves men is loved by them; he who respects them is, in turn, respected. Let us suppose that having behaved discourteously or rudely toward us; if we are prudent, the first thing we must ask ourselves is if we have previously committed any discourtesy with such a person or if we have been unfair to him; his attitude toward us must have some foundation. If we come to the conclusion that we have not done any injustice to such a person, but have always shown ourselves to him kind and courteous, we must continue to analyze the possible causes of discourteous or rude attitude. If we are prudent, we must reflect whether we have committed the slightest impropriety in our conduct. Assuming that we have not committed any wrongdoing either, then the discourtesy or rudeness of the offended one is utterly unfounded, and the prudent man, faced with such a situation, must conclude:

"This man is but an extravagant and a fool; he is nothing different from a beast, in which case, why should I care about the attitude or acts of a beast?".

To enjoy prestige and consideration is one of the things which men crave most ardently.

The first and foremost duty of filial piety is to honour our parents properly. The best proof of this love for parents is to provide them with the necessary sustenance.

He could not do it by means of words, because Heaven does not speak. Heaven manifests its will through the merits and good deeds of men. This is the only way He manifests His will. Heaven sees through the eyes of the people; Heaven hears through the ears of the people.

Heaven governs the events of the world without being seen; this occult action of Heaven is what is called "Destiny".

I have never heard that a man who did not act with righteousness managed to straighten others. Still less could he make others sincere who observe hypocritical behaviour.

Ministers are known by the people they welcome into their home when they are in court, and by the houses in which they are housed when they are out of court.

In order for true friendship to develop, it is necessary to dispense with the superiority that age, honours, riches, or power may bestow. The only motive that should incite us to friendship is the search for virtues and mutual perfection.

The superior must honour and respect the wisdom of his subjects, and the inferior must be respectful and courteous to his superiors, in attention to the dignity they hold; respecting dignity and honouring the wise are two manifestations of the same duty.

He who, in order to remain faithful to his principles, refuses to be elevated to an honourable condition remains happy even without honours. who, in order not to stray from the right path, rejects a certain income, remains joyful in his poverty.

Human nature is neither good nor bad. According to this, the goodness or malice of men is something subsequent to their own human nature in its origin. If man has the capacity to act, it is necessary that he also has a norm to direct his acts.

If the supreme good of man consisted in preserving life, he would do nothing but dedicate himself to discovering and practicing all that could prolong it. If the most fearsome evil of man were death, he would investigate and practice everything that could keep him away or prevent this evil. There are things that we love more than life, just as there are things more fearsome than death; this is a feeling common to all men.

The straight path is like a wide avenue; it is not difficult to find when one seeks it, but men do not strive to discover it.

When the wise man makes a determination, it is

impossible for the people to penetrate into the true motives of it. When a prince is surrounded by perverse men, sycophants and serve them, can he govern wisely and effectively?

When Heaven wants to give someone a difficult mission, it first tests the strength of their spirit and the balance of their mind with the difficulties of a hard life; it fatigues their muscles and their whole body with hard work, which tests their endurance; it mortifies their flesh and skin with the rigors of hunger and cold; it subjects them to the greatest deprivations of misery; it determines that they will not succeed in their undertakings so that they will face failure. In this way, heaven stimulates their virtues, strengthens their bodies and makes them apt to face the difficulties they will encounter in the fulfilment of their high mission. Difficulty is what most stimulates man to overcome his deficiencies and overcome them.

Only when all kinds of privations and works have been suffered, only when the face of misery has been seen, only then is it possible to know human nature in depth.

Man fulfils the will of Heaven when he strives to perfect himself.

If you seek you will find, if you are negligent you will lose everything. He who seeks what is within him will discover it and attain it; the success of this search is certain; an invariable law guarantees the acquisition of what is sought. If, on the other hand, we seek what is outside us, all efforts will be fruitless.

The origin of all actions lies within our being. If,

reflecting on our own acts, we discover that they are in conformity with our rational nature; we will experience the most intense satisfaction.

Man cannot but repent of his faults. If once he repents of not having repented of his faults, he will no longer have cause for repentance.

The people do not value the merit of a good ruler. The good ruler leads the people towards good by his presence alone; his action is hidden and imperceptible like that of the spirits. The influence of his virtue is felt everywhere, like that of the subtle forces of heaven and earth. The influence of a good ruler has no limits.

Examples of goodness penetrate the hearts of men more deeply than good words; it is easier to obtain the affection of the people by right action and right advice than by effective administration and just laws. The people distrust laws and administration; the people love good examples and good counsels. Fair laws and efficient administration increase the revenue of the kingdom; with good teachings and good examples the heart of the subjects is won.

Penalties and privations sharpen intelligence and strengthen prudence.

No one should eat without having earned it.

The ways of the wise are high and inaccessible. His deeds may be admired, but not imitated.

The skilful carpenter does not become clumsy in order to be imitated by any of his assistants.

He who abstains from what he should not abstain from is better to abstain from everything; he who treats with coldness those who should treat with tenderness will end up treating the whole world with coldness; those who advance hastily will also retreat with the same precipitation.

It is better to ignore historical books than to accept unconditionally what is referred to in them.

To kill a close relative of another man is the crime that causes the direst consequences.

I do not pay the slightest attention to the murmurings and criticisms of men.

In order that our words may always be in conformity with fairness, it is necessary to avoid excessive familiarity with those around us; mutual respect is the best defence against discourteous and coarse words. If the learned man speaks when he should be silent, all are perplexed at his words; if, on the contrary, the learned man is silent when he should speak, all are bewildered at his silence.

The best words are those that have a profound meaning and, at the same time, are comprehensible to the whole world.

The greatest defect of men consists in worrying about uprooting the tares from the fields of others, neglecting the cultivation of their own fields.

The best way to attain the virtues of justice and equity is to dominate passions. He who allows himself to be dominated by passions is very difficult to act with justice and equity.

Every man must do his duty, regardless of what others may say of his conduct. Those who act solely to merit the approval of other men can be regarded as the flatterers of the world; these are the men of apparent virtue who are now regarded as the most honest.

****Mencius, Meng Ke or Master Meng (370-289 B.C.) is regarded as the most notable follower of Confucian ideas. To him is attributed the extreme defence that man is good by nature, so that in every man are manifested tendencies or feelings that can lead him on the right path, such as feelings of compassion, shame, modesty and the ability to discern between good and evil. He adds that these feelings can be cultivated as a plant whose fruits are ethical values or virtues: such as benevolence, righteousness, and wisdom, among others. By their nature, these notions differ to some extent from the later ideas of Machiavelli or Darwin in this regard.

ANNEX II.

SOME OBSERVATIONS ON THE WAY OF ACTING OF CONFUCIUS.

Confucius, in his native town, was simple and unpretentious. He did not seem to be a good orator.

In the temple of his ancestors and in the court, he spoke fluently, but with a certain reserve.

In court, he spoke to ministers of lower rank with frankness and affability. To those of higher rank, he spoke calmly, but decisively.

In the presence of his Sovereign, he seemed full of fear, but at the same time serious and withdrawn.

When the Prince used him to receive distinguished visitors, his expression changed and his legs bent. Standing in the presence of the visitors, he waved with his hands clasped, turning from left to right and with his suit tightly fitted. Then he went forward with his arms outstretched like the wings of a bird.

As he returned from the audience and descended the first step, his face lost the expression of anxiety and seemed serene and happy. When he reached the end of the steps, he hurried off with his arms outstretched like wings; but when he returned to his place, he still seemed full of fear.

He wore the Prince's badges with his body slightly bent, as if he could hardly bear his weight; he lifted them to the height of his head and lowered them again to the height of his chest. His face indicated nervousness, and he dragged his feet as if something were holding them to the ground.

Offering presents as an ambassador, his appearance was quiet.

In a private audience, his face was always smiling.

He did not eat badly cut or served meat without the proper sauce. Even though there was an abundance of meat, he never allowed it to outbid vegetables.

He didn't drink wine with limitation, but he never got into a state of drunkenness.

He didn't eat much.

When he ate, he didn't talk; when he was in bed, he didn't talk.

Although he had nothing but common rice and vegetable soup, he always offered something with reverence to the ancestral spirits.

He did not sit on a poorly laid carpet.

Having sent him Chi K'ang Tzu some medicine, he bowed to receive it, saying: not being accustomed to this drug, I do not dare to try it.

His stables having been burned, the Master asked as he returned from court:

Has anyone been injured? He did not ask for the horses.

If the Prince called him to his presence, he went on foot without waiting for his chariot.

If any of his friends died without a house or relatives, he offered to attend the funerals.

In bed, he did not lie like a corpse.

At home, his ways were not studied.

In the sight of a person in mourning, even if he was a close friend, he always showed himself to be serious.

In his moments of rest, the Master was generally cheerful and smiling.

If the Master had to eat with one who mourned for his parents, he could not finish the meal.

He never sang during the day he had attended a duel.

The Master never spoke of prodigies, of feats of strength, of crimes, nor of supernatural beings.

The Master taught mainly four things: Knowledge of literature and arts, Conduct, Equity, and Truth.

The Master fished with a rod and not with a net.

When he went out with a bow and arrow, he only wounded the birds in the wing.
If the Master was with singers and they sang well, he urged them to repeat singing himself with them.

The Master was affable, but serious; severe, but not harsh; attentive in his conduct, but not calm.

There were four words that the Master never used: I will, you must, surely, and me.

When the Master saw a person in mourning, in ceremonial attire, or blind, he immediately rose from his seat, even if it was a person younger than himself; if he found her in the street, he would hasten his step.

When he met an officer in uniform, or a blind man, although dressed in rags, he always made a gesture of respect.

When a rich banquet was offered to him, he rose to give thanks, showing his appreciation in the countenance.

He changed his countenance when he heard thunder or a howl of wind.

When he was in a car, he didn't look back, he didn't speak quickly, and he didn't point.

OTHER BOOKS BY THE AUTHOR

-Confucius vs. Machiavelli (In Hispanish)

-The Political Code of Confucius

-The Education Code of Confucius

-Confucius to Confusing

-A requiem for Machiavelli (In Hispanish)

BIBLIOGRAPHY

Adler, J. (2011). *Confucianism in China Today.* Pearson Living Religions Forum New York April 14, 2011.

Aguilar, J. (2010*). Los cuatro libros clásicos del Confucianismo: una lectura conómica.* Rev. Empresa y Humanismo Vol. XIII, 2/10, pp. 13-40.

Arnaiz, Ch. (2014). *Confucianismo, Budismo y la Conformación de valores en China.* Inst. Gino Germani. Nov. 2014.

Ataide y Portugal. Librería del Castillo. (1802). *Vida y pensamientos morales de Confucio.* (Old Classic).

Bailey, P. (2001). *China in the Twentieth Century.* Editor digital: Betatron (2001).

Balazs, E. (1975). *La burocracia celeste; historia de la China imperial.* Barcelona, Seix Barral, 1975.

Bauer, W. (2006).Geschichte der chinesischen Philosophie. Hans van Ess.

Bedi, S. (2009). *Rejecting Rights.* Cambridge University Press 2009.

Botton, F. (2000). *China: Su historia y cultura hasta 1800.* México, D.F. El Colegio de México.

Capra, F. (2005). *El Tao de la Física. Una*

exploración de los paralelismos entre la física moderna y el misticismo oriental, Editorial Sirio, Barcelona. 2005.

Carrasco, M. (2011). *Confucio y la Educación*. CHIR Nº 67, 01 de Octubre de, 2011

Cham, S. (2004). *Liberalism, Democracy and Developmen*. Cambridge University Press.

Cheng, A. (2011), *Virtue and Politics: Some conceptions of sovereignty in Ancient China*, Journal of Chinese Philosophy, No. 38, pp. 113-145.

Cheng, Chung-Ying. (2011). *New Confucianism as a Philosophy of Humanity and Governance*. Journal of Chinese Philosophy, No. 38, pp. 1 y 2.

Creel-Herrle. (1976), *El pensamiento chino desde Confucio hasta Mao Tze Tung*. Edit. Alianza, Madrid.1976.

Colegio de México. (2002). *La interpretación Ricciana del Confucianismo*. Estudios de Asia y África, Vol. XXVII, núm. 2, mayo-agosto, 2002, pp. 211-239. El Colegio de México, A.C.

Confucio; (1998). *Los cuatro libros de la sabiduría*, Edicomunicación S.A., España, 1998.

Confucio. (2014). *Los cuatro libros*. Traducción y notas. J. Arroyo. PAIDÓS, Barcelona (2014).

Confucio. (1997*). Analectas.* Traducción, edición y notas A. Suárez, Madrid: Kairós.

Confucio. *El TAO-HIO o Gran Estudio*. Texto de Confucio y Comentario de Thseng-Tseu.

Dawson, R. et al. (1967). *El legado de China*. Edit. Pegaso, Madrid, 1967.

De Bary, W. (1998). *Confucianism and Human Rights. Introduction* In De Bary William T., y Weiming, Tu (eds.), Nueva York: Columbia University Press, pp. 1-26.

De Prada, A. (2013). *Confucianismo y Democracia: Ciudadanos, príncipes, individuos*. Universidad Rey Juan Carlos. ISEGORÍA. Revista de Filosofía Moral y Política. N° 49, julio-diciembre, 2013, 615-627.

Doval, G. (2011): *Breve historia de la china milenaria*, Madrid, Nautilus.

Feldherr, A. and G. Hardy. (2011). *The Oxford history the historical Writing*. Vol 1. Beginnings to BC 600. Oxford University Press.

Ferrater, J. (1954). *Diccionario de Filosofía*. T I. 5ta. Edic, Editorial Sudaméricana.

Folch, D. (2001). La *construcción de China. El período formativo de la civilización china*. Península/Atalaya, Barcelona 2001.

Franke, H. y R. Trauzettel (1973). *El imperio chino*. Trad.: M. Moya. Siglo XXI, Madrid, 1973.

Fung, Y. (1997). *A short history of Chinese Philosophy*. Nueva York, Free Press.

García, I. (2017). *Confucio y el mundo que viene.* Documento Análisis, ieee.es 24/2017

Granet, M. (1959*).* *El pensamiento chino.* Trad. V. Clavel. Edit.UTEHA, Mexico 1959.

Grousset, R. (1958*).* *Historia de la China.* Edit. Caralt, Barcelona. 1958.

Guirao, P. (1927). *El evangelio de Confucio (Analectas de Confucio*). Barcelona, 1927.

Hang, L. (2011). *Traditional Confucianism and its Contemporary Relevance,* Asian Philosophy, 21(4), pp. 437-445.

Höffe, O. (2003) *Breve historia ilustrada de la filosofía.* Ediciones Península, Barcelona.

Hucker, Ch. (1975). *China's Imperial Past: An Introduction to Chinese History and Culture.* Stanford University Press, 1975.

John Parratt. Edit. (2004). *An Introduction to Third World Theologies.* Edit. Cambridge University Press

KAILAS (2014). *Analectas Confucio.* Kailas Edit. Junio 2014.

Kung, H. (1991). *Proyecto de una ética mundial.* Edit. Trotta, Madrid, 1991.

Kung-Kuan, J. (1965). *Confucio educador.* Diana, artes Gráficas, 1965.

Lau, D. (1979). *Lún Yu, Confucius, The Analects.*

Penguin Books. 1979.

Lao Zi (1981). El libro del Tao, Alfaguara, Madrid.

Lemus, D. (2014), *Confucianismo como humanidad: Claves para complementar la modernidad.* México y la Cuenca del Pacífico. Sept.-Dic. (2014).

Leys, S. (1998). *Confucio: Analectas, versión y notas.* EDAF. Madrid.

Li-Jing. Clásicos chinos Confucianos de la Antigüedad. Tratado de los ritos. Vol I (libros 1-8).

Liqing, Q. and M. Shangchao. (2009). *A Study on Confucius' Views on Language Functions.* Polyglossia Vol. 16, February 2009.

López, C. y R. Rouco. (2016). *Confucio para Corruptos Confusos.* Creative People, May. Lic 4.0, 2016.

López, C. y R. Rouco. (2016). *Confucio para Confusos.* Amazons KDP Publishing, Junio de 2016. ISBN 9781520894621.

McGraw Hill. (2001). Gran Diccionario Enciclopédico Ilustrado. Edit. McGraw Hill Interamericano.

McLeisk K. Edit. (1993). *Key Ideas in Human.* Thought Library of Congress Cataloging-in-Publication Data. New York. 1993.

Menander, Dawson Miles, (1915). *The Ethics of Confucius.* Whith A Foreword by Wu Ting Fang. G.

P. Putnam's Sons. The knickerborker {press). New York and London (1915).

Peerenboom, R. (1998). *Confucian Harmony and Freedom of Thought*. In De Bary William T., y Weiming, Tu (eds.), Confucianism and Human Rights, Nueva York: Columbia University Press, pp. 234-260.

Perceval, J. y J. Fornieles. (2008). *Confucio contra Sócrates*. Análisis 36: 213-224

Pérez Arroyo. (2006). *Confucio*. Ediciones RBA, Barcelona. 2006

R.A.E. Diccionario de la Real Academia Española.

Robert Audi. Edit. (1999). *The Cambridge Dictionary of Philosophy*. Second Edition. Edit..Cambridge University Press. 1999.

Ronan C. (1978). *The Shorter Sciense and Civilisation in China* Vol 1. Cambridge University Press.

Schleichert, H. y H. Roetz. (2013). *Filosofía china clásica*. Traducción de A. Peñataro. Herder, Barcelona 2013.

Stratern, P. (2004). Confucio en 90 minutos. Casa del libro, España.

Ted Honderich. Edit. (2005). *The Oxford Companion of Philosophy*. Second Edition. Oxford University Press. 2005.

Tu, W. (1998). *Confucius and Confucianism*. In Slote, Walter H., and Devos, George A. (eds.), Confucianism and the Family, Nueva York: Suny Press, pp. 3-36.

Waley, A. (1938). *The Analects of Confucius*: George Allen & Unwin, Londres, 1938.

Wang Lei. (2007). *A study on Confucius' rectification of names*. Information of Culture and Education, 2: 92-93.

Watts, A. (1976). *El camino del Tao*. Kairos, Barcelona, 1976.

Wright, A. (ed.). (1960). *The Confucian Persuasion*. Stanford, Stanford University Press, 1960.

Wilhelm, R. *Confucio*. (1966). Trad.: A. García. Madrid, Madrid, 1966

Xinzhong Yao. (2000). An Introduction to Confucianism. Cambridge University Press. (2000).

Xinzhong Yao; (2001), *The Confucianism*. The Press Syndicate of the University of   Cambridge, 2001.

Yang, B. *Lunyu Yizhu*. (1958).   Pekín: Zhonghua Shuju 1958.

Zhang, T. and B.Schwartz. (1997). *Confucius and the Cultural Revolution: A Study in Collective Memory*, International Journal of Politics, Culture and Society, 11(2), pp. 189-211.

Zhao Z. (2014). *Confucio. Ética y Civilización*.

Revista Co-herencia. V. 10 No. 20. Enero-junio 2014.
Medellín, Colombia.

ÍNDEX

-Author's foreword .... pag. 003

I.-Introduction. Our Time .... pag. 008

II.-The not Confused Ethics of Confucius. pag. 014

III.-Ethical Values in Confucius Aphorisms..p. 019

IV.-Confucius Aphorisms on Ethics and
      Morals .... pag. 039

-Appendix .... pag. 067

-Annex I. Confucius, The Four Classical
   Books .... pag. 072

-Annex II. Some Observations on the way
  of acting Confucius........................   pag. 102

-Other books by the author. ....pag. 106

-Bibliograpy .... pag. 107

-Index .... pag. 115

115